MAKING SCHOOL
REFORM WORK

MAKING SCHOOL REFORM WORK

New Partnerships for Real Change

PAUL T. HILL

JAMES HARVEY

editors

BROOKINGS INSTITUTION PRESS

Washington, D.C.

Copyright © 2004
THE BROOKINGS INSTITUTION
1775 Massachusetts Avenue, N.W., Washington, D.C. 20036
www.brookings.edu

Library of Congress Cataloging-in-Publication data

Making school reform work : new partnerships for real change / Paul T. Hill and James Harvey, editors.
   p. cm.
Includes bibliographical references and index.
ISBN 0-8157-3641-X (pbk. : alk. paper)
   1. School improvement programs—United States. 2. Community and school—United States. 3. Business and education—United States. 4. Education, Urban—United States. I. Hill, Paul Thomas, 1943– II. Harvey, James, 1944– III. Brookings Institution. IV. Title.
   LB2822.82.M35 2004
   371.2'00973—dc22   2004016554

9 8 7 6 5 4 3 2 1
The paper used in this publication meets minimum requirements of the American National Standard for Information Sciences—Permanence of Paper for Printed Library Materials: ANSI Z39.48-1992.

Typeset in Sabon

Composition by Stephen D. McDougal
Mechanicsville, Maryland

Printed by R. R. Donnelley
Harrisonburg, Virginia

Contents

Foreword

IN 1997, RECOGNIZING that big city public school systems were continuing to struggle despite more than a decade of reform initiatives, Brookings and its Brown Center on Education Policy set out to create new, more powerful options for city leaders. We designed our work to help mayors and leaders of business and philanthropy as well as school boards and superintendents. Brookings nonresident senior fellow Paul T. Hill, a professor at the University of Washington's Daniel J. Evans School of Public Affairs, led the work. The effort was funded by the Alcoa Foundation, the Smith Richardson Foundation, the Pew Charitable Trusts, the Edna McConnell Clark Foundation, and the Joyce Foundation.

This is the third and final book to emerge from Brookings's urban public education initiative. Our first book, *Fixing Urban Schools* (1998), analyzed the proposed strategies for urban education reform, including standards, teacher training, school chartering, and vouchers, and showed that each addressed only a subset of the problems that urban public education must overcome. It concluded that effective reform initiatives must both strengthen existing public schools and create independent options that would compete with existing schools and create choices for families stuck in unproductive schools.

The second book, *It Takes a City* (2000), studied reform initiatives in cities considered at the time to be making the most progress toward school improvement. It reported that none of the cities' reform strategies was as deeply thought through or as well implemented as advertised. Even relatively weak reform initiatives, when implemented, were often abandoned

vii

as soon as their effects on the work of teachers and administrators stimulated resistance.

It Takes a City concluded that reform initiatives strong enough to change the overall quality of public education in a city must combine three elements:

—Incentives to reward good performance and sanction bad, including giving families choices so that people and resources can move from less- to more-successful providers of instruction;

—Investments in capacity, to encourage new approaches and ideas that can be optioned by educators and parents; and

—School freedom of action, so that people with new ideas about how to use money, children's and teachers' time, and instructional methods can put them into practice and also abandon their own practices in favor of better ones they see elsewhere.

The book also concluded that school boards and superintendents are too politically vulnerable and unstable to implement deep and lasting change. It suggested that communities need new leadership structures with wider constituencies than the teachers union and PTA and that reform requires institutional capacities that school districts are unlikely to develop. *It Takes a City* ended with the promise of a third book, one that would show city leaders how they could construct civic coalitions that could build and sustain effective reform strategies, and how cities could build other institutional capacities necessary for reform.

This new book fulfills the promise made at the end of *It Takes a City*. It explains why cities need to create stronger leadership and deeper capacities than school districts can provide and shows how they can do it. The seven chapters, all written by research staff members at the University of Washington's Center on Reinventing Public Education, show how cities can create

—Long-lasting civic reform oversight groups to formulate and sustain support for reforms;

—Incubators to create new schools;

—Real estate trusts to break the school district's monopoly on school buildings and find facilities for new schools;

—Independent institutions to analyze school performance data and report on the progress and sticking points of reform;

—Ways to strengthen the teaching force by attracting teachers from among the ablest college graduates;

—New ways to identify and develop principals who can lead schools in an environment of performance pressure and competition for students; and

—Inspectorates that can diagnose schools' performance more richly than is possible via test scores alone.

Volume editors Paul Hill and James Harvey conclude the book by defining the "third way philanthropy"—by which foundations and businesses help public education by creating institutional capacities that school districts need but cannot provide for themselves—and estimating the costs of such institutions in a typical metropolitan area.

Brookings is proud of this book and the work that has led to it. It helps fulfill our commitment to developing constructive new ideas that serve the public interest.

STROBE TALBOTT
President
Brookings Institution

August 2004
Washington, D.C.

MAKING SCHOOL
REFORM WORK

ONE *A Fresh Assessment:*
Why Reform
Initiatives Fail

PAUL T. HILL
JAMES HARVEY

AS THE 1990S DAWNED, the outlook for genuine,
deep-rooted school reform had never looked better. Under the leadership
of President George H. W. Bush and Governor Bill Clinton of Arkansas,
the nation's governors had adopted six impressive National Education
Goals. Business leaders, rallied by the Business Roundtable and the National Alliance for Business, had thrown their weight behind the goals. A
coalition of corporate and philanthropic interests was busy cobbling together an ambitious effort to reshape schools, the New American Schools
Development Corporation. And a consensus was developing around "systemic" reform, a catch-all educational buzzword emphasizing the "alignment" of standards, curriculum, assessment, textbooks and materials, and
teacher training. On balance, things looked pretty good.

This activity grew out of, and built on, a prior decade of reform, one
launched by the seminal report of the National Commission on Excellence in Education, *A Nation at Risk*. Based on that document's startling
assertion that a "rising tide of mediocrity" in public and private schools
threatened the nation's educational foundations, federal and state leaders
chivied local educators into paying more attention to standards. Corporate America shouldered its part of the burden through thousands of "partnerships" with local schools. Philanthropists, ranging from the Carnegie
Foundation to the Twentieth Century Fund, financed impressive analyses
of what needed to be done or offered their own suggestions. And leaders
across the board agreed that education had finally assumed its rightful
spot at the top of the nation's domestic agenda.

I

As the United States moves into the first decade of a new millennium, the interest in school improvement remains high. President George W. Bush and his secretary of education, Rod Paige, have succeeded in enacting the No Child Left Behind program. Working with Senator Edward M. Kennedy of Massachusetts, they have produced legislation tying standards and annual assessments to federal aid to children in low-income schools. The business community, rallied by Louis V. Gerstner Jr., chairman and CEO of IBM, has worked with the nation's governors to create ACHIEVE, an organization dedicated to standards-based reform. And a new array of philanthropists, prominently featuring the Bill and Melinda Gates Foundation, which did not exist when *A Nation at Risk* appeared, has set out to reshape school district administration and the American high school. Whenever the representatives of these interests gather together, they tend to agree that things are getting better, although the work is difficult and progress is slow, and that leaders must stay the course.

The truth is that, after two decades of well-publicized effort, public school systems in the United States remain about where they were in 1983, particularly those systems in urban areas. When progress can be discerned, it is fragmentary, fragile, and confined almost exclusively to the elementary school years. Middle schools have barely changed at all, and high schools have become the black hole of reform, into which good ideas are sucked, never to be seen again. Two enormous problems that have characterized big-city schools for years—a troubling achievement gap between minority and white students and high school dropout rates hovering around 50 percent for Hispanic and African American students—remain essentially unchanged.

The abysmally poor performance of urban schools led the Brookings Institution in 1997 to commit to a five-year initiative on big-city school reform. The initiative started with a simple question. "What could we say to mayors or civic leaders who asked how they could turn around a low-performing urban school district?" To this point, the initiative has produced two books. The first, *Fixing Urban Schools*, examined popular school reform proposals of the 1990s, critiqued their weaknesses, and suggested how different approaches could be combined into more potent strategies for whole-system change. The second, *It Takes a City*, drew on the experience of efforts in several cities to suggest how communities could build political support and implementation capacity for deep and lasting reform of public education.[1]

Near the end of *It Takes A City*, the authors argued that most school districts neglect activities that are necessary for powerful and long-lasting reform. The day-to-day imperatives facing school boards, the need to pay teachers, keep schools operating, and support the central office, lead to starving many activities essential to long-term improvement.[2] Moreover, the urge to avoid controversy and limit scrutiny discourages close tracking of performance, including checks on whether announced reforms have even been implemented, never mind succeeded.

This third and final book explores the need for such activities. It reflects on what the Brookings initiative has learned about the capacity of reformers to realize their ambitions. Unlike the first two books, this edited book of essays focuses on what is needed to ensure that the reform objectives defined by leaders are translated into real change.

The impetus for this volume rests on three streams of thought. It began with a sense that existing systems needed more bells and whistles if reform were to succeed. So the first stream of thought was simply that reform will not happen if left to school systems themselves to implement. But that concept changed over time as the authors became convinced that the system of schooling in the United States rejects change in much the same way that the human body fights transplants. Just as hospitals administer medicines and powerful agents to suppress the body's natural immune system, so too schools need independent institutions to help fight off rejection of change, maintain the environment for reform, and provide support at critical moments. These institutions should be friendly to the public schools and sympathetic to their aims but separate from them. Only then can the public be sure that important reforms will be developed, will be implemented deeply and thoroughly, and will survive long enough to make a difference.

The second stream of thought was the authors' realization that public schools in the United States have never been subjected to the structured and structural scrutiny routinely applied in the private sector and even in government. Regardless of what one thinks of the "quality improvement movement" in American industry or the "reinventing government" initiative of the Clinton administration, the fact remains that, in the context of respecting the broad missions of their respective sectors, these activities set out to improve important private and public capabilities. The quality improvement gurus never questioned the profit motive, just as the reinventing government initiatives did not take issue with the function of the government as a provider and guarantor of services. Each sought to improve the likelihood that these missions would be accomplished.

What was novel about them was that each set out to explore whether clarifying goals or modifying existing ways of doing business would accomplish the mission better. Is the goal of employment training simply to help people find work? Support family well-being? Or strengthen local communities? If reformers are required to focus on just one of those goals, what would that mean for how the local Office of Employment Security operates? Does Ford Motor Company exist to compete with General Motors? To protect market share from foreign imports? Or to ensure customer satisfaction? If one focuses on competition with General Motors, does that necessarily protect market share or improve customer satisfaction? Although much public comment about quality improvement has focused on statistical process controls and measuring progress, the initial step always requires clarifying purpose.

The reality is that purposes are never singular but always plural. Job training provides jobs, supports families, and generates wealth and economic development. An automobile manufacturer is simultaneously intent on competing with domestic rivals, fending off imports, and satisfying customers. A one-purpose approach invites mistakes, something Joseph Chamberlain Wilson, a former president of the Haloid Company that turned into Xerox, understood intuitively. When Wilson died in 1971, a tattered index card was found in his wallet summarizing his goals in life to include: "to attain serenity . . . through leadership of a business which brings happiness to its workers, serves well its customers and brings prosperity to its owners."[3] The Haloid Xerox approach, like that of Ford Motor Company or the federal government, accepted several purposes as legitimate, understanding that the art of leadership lies in clarifying the purposes and their comparative significance and relationship to one another.

Schools too have many purposes. And the tension among them is not resolved by focusing on one and ignoring the others. Parents (and citizens) maintain an unspoken bottom line about schools. Children should be safe in them. A standards-based reform movement cannot afford to be seen as cavalierly ignoring that concern. Parents also want schools to help their students develop as children and mature through adolescence. Assessment advocates cannot turn a deaf ear to that anxiety. And parents and community leaders want students to achieve at the highest possible levels. School leaders must pay more than lip service to this purpose, resisting the temptation to point to dysfunctional urban neighborhoods and chaotic home situations to explain students' poor performance or high dropout rates.

So the question naturally arises, how should traditional school governance practice be modified in light of various school purposes, new demands for performance, and the accelerating pace of change of recent decades? This is an age, for example, in which more than two-thirds of high school graduates continue their education immediately out of high school. Recently, college women have enjoyed unlimited access to entry-level employment in business and the professions. Employment security in the private sector (and often the public) has become a thing of the past. And most college-educated workers can be expected to cycle through up to seven different occupations in their careers. In this environment, do school personnel practices inherited from the past still make sense? Is a teacher training system invented a century ago so that rural white girls could find work within a few miles of their parents' home good enough?[4] Or do we need something more? Should schools be thinking of new ways of training, hiring, and replacing teachers, not because there is anything pernicious about the inheritance, but because times have changed and schools need to change with them?

School leaders genuflect when the idea of modifying the way schools do their work is brought up, but change is almost never put on the table in a serious way. Schools continue, for the most part, to be seen as public institutions, staffed by public servants, overseen by public employees, in facilities owned and managed by public agencies. The political dynamics appear to require accepting current structures as the natural order of things. Reform in this framework is something that is welcome as long as it changes nothing of major consequence to the adults in the system.

The third stream was the authors' realization that it has become painfully obvious after two decades of reform that the system of schooling in the United States seems incapable of change even if the need for it is based on its experience and noted on its research and development agenda. American schools, like sick patients whose bodies reject the transplants that might save their lives, treat change as a foreign body. National and state leaders, public and private, join this conspiracy of silence about persistent failure. Whether through hubris or ignorance, generation after generation of public and private leaders enter the operating room apparently unaware that the procedure failed the last time it was tried—and the time before, as well.

In the face of the transparent abandonment of successful and functioning New American Schools models, as soon as the superintendents who had championed them moved on or were shoved out, for example, why not pretend that another round of model development would make the difference? And so, efforts to create small schools and reshape the high school took center stage as the new millennium dawned, despite the palpable failure of earlier school-model development efforts, dating back to the Experimental Schools and Model Schools programs developed in the heyday of President Lyndon B. Johnson's Great Society.[5]

If earlier efforts have not worked out, they can be conveniently ignored. This helps explain why the National Education Goals, developed with great fanfare in 1989 and discussed enthusiastically by public and private leaders through the early 1990s, were put on a shelf as the decade grew to a close. Faced with troubling evidence about scandalously high minority dropout rates, the stagnation of reading scores in urban elementary schools, and low math and science achievement among high school students, why remind people of ten-year-old promises to fix dropout rates, make sure children entered school ready to read, and produce American graduates who would be first in the world in math and science? The goals were best consigned to the memory hole of school reform. And for the most part, they have been. Nobody talks about them anymore. The topic of conversation has changed to "leaving no child behind."

Drawing on these three streams of thought, therefore, this book, unlike the earlier two, relies less on analysis of what is than on imagining what might be. It explores some alternative ways public schools might pursue their mission.

This book outlines the shape of needed institutions that are not limited by conventional educators' willingness to change and defines two classes of institutions: community leadership structures and technical capacities. Community leadership structures can formulate and sustain reform strategies that are more ambitious and likely to benefit poor children than anything conventional school administrators are likely to formulate. And communities are likely to need technical capacities, which school districts cannot create or sustain, to improve their schools. Individual localities will inevitably find some of these ideas more attractive than others. However, the main message of this book is applicable everywhere: public education in big cities needs new community-based leadership, strategies, and investment. We have already tried investment without a coherent strategy (for example, compensatory education), and strategy without investment (for example, national goals and statewide standards), and now the nation appears poised to emphasize the need for leadership largely without regard to strategy or investment. In all those cases the result is activity without deep or lasting benefits. Effective school reform requires putting the three elements together.

Notes

1. Paul T. Hill and Mary Beth Celio, *Fixing Urban Schools* (Brookings, 1998); and Paul T. Hill, Christine Campbell, and James Harvey, *It Takes a City: Getting Serious about Urban School Reform* (Brookings, 2000).

2. In a series of confidential interviews conducted by the authors with school superintendents and chief financial officers, most said that efforts to improve instruction were constrained by the fact that funds are all tied up in salaries for incumbent teachers and compliance with mandates from courts and the federal and state governments.

3. David T. Kearns and David Nadler, *Prophets in the Dark: How Xerox Reinvented Itself and Beat Back the Japanese* (HarperCollins, 1992).

4. Martin Haberman, *Finding (and Keeping) Great Teachers*, Highlights of the Missouri Superintendents Forum, 2001 (Kansas City: Ewing Marion Kauffman Foundation, 2002).

5. The editors of this volume helped to shape and develop the New American Schools effort from the outset. They were also involved in selecting the "design teams" developing new school models. Although everyone vowed to avoid repeating the mistakes made earlier by the Experimental Schools and Model Schools programs, in fact, precisely the same mistakes were made.

TWO *The Need for*
New Institutions

PAUL T. HILL

NO ONE CAN SAY exactly what configuration of
schools and other educational programs will ultimately solve the problem
of ineffective public education in big cities. Clearly existing school districts and the schools they provide are not succeeding. And clearly the
groups with the most influence over school district policy do not see ex-
perimenting and adapting until effective ways of providing instruction
are found as the way to solve the problem. Instead, despite public pro-
nouncements in support of improving student achievement and doing
whatever is necessary to advance it, the real political dynamics in most
urban areas revolve around protecting the jobs of adults.

Recent significant concerns about federal assistance for schools in low-
income areas indicate that this judgment is not too harsh. One major result of providing federal funds for the education of low-income children
for the past thirty-five years has been the establishment of a well-
protected employment service for teachers' aides, many without teaching
credentials or college degrees.[1]

The need for new independent capacities stems from the deficiencies of
school district governance. It is not too much to say that although everyone can agree in public that the mission of the schools is the education of
children, the goal of governance, in private, pivots on satisfying the needs
of adults. In district after district, for example, racial tension among school
board members about the ethnicity of a new superintendent is often ex-
pressed as a concern about the "openness" of the selection process or a
preference that a new superintendent represent one of the dominant eth-

nic groups in the community. Doubtless, both concerns have some validity. But what is never mentioned in public is that, in most big cities, public schools are one of the biggest employers in the community—often the major employer. Whoever presides over this system is responsible for thousands of jobs, sometimes tens of thousands of positions, all stable and relatively well paying with exceptional benefits. No elected public official, on a school board or elsewhere in the city, can afford to ignore how those jobs are filled, especially when 50 percent of them turn over every five years.

It is perhaps inevitable that although their ultimate goal is students' learning, school districts work toward that goal through alignments of adults. Citizens are represented on the school board; parents' preferences about instruction are promised a hearing; and unions protect teachers. Teachers are further shielded by guarantees of various kinds written into state laws, local contracts, and the "contracts behind the contract," or special language and agreements worked out around the contract.[2] Many other district employees are also provided with job protections, often through unions representing, for example, bus drivers or cafeteria employees.

One effect of these adult agreements is that equity and fairness often take a back seat to seniority and tenure. In practically every school district in the country, funds are not allocated to schools on a per student basis but are used to support teachers' salaries. The lion's share of district operating funds, therefore, is spent with an implicit understanding that little or nothing can be done about the fact that the best-paid teachers with the most seniority get their pick of teaching assignments in the "most attractive" schools. This understanding effectively consigns the most inexperienced, junior, and least well-paid teachers to schools with the greatest challenges. In truly democratic building trades unions, by contrast, lists of skilled members needing work are maintained. When a new job comes into the hiring hall, the first name on the list is offered the job, whether that carpenter has just completed apprentice school or has years as a journeyman. None of the adults connected with a public school system is indifferent to whether children are taught well. But all of them impose constraints on the way things are done.

Meanwhile, even among public institutions, public schools seem peculiarly impervious to what is going on around them. In the private sector, and even state and federal government, effective CEOs and managers understand that protecting the institution for which they are responsible (and the divergent interests of stockholders, customers, and employees) demands paying attention to social, economic, and demographic changes. Although outstanding leadership in the corporate world is as scarce as it is in the public sector, the best leaders do not hesitate to gauge new markets, test new products, reshape how they produce widgets or provide services, abandon unproductive product lines, and offer specialized services and products to meet boutique requests and niche demands. The largest national employer in the private sector is not a manufacturing giant or even one of the new high-technology leviathans of the last quarter century. It is a temporary services employment agency, Manpower, Inc., offering on-demand, specialized skills, when they are required, wherever they are required.

Against the backdrop of this nimbleness and adaptability in the private sector, school management seems left behind when it comes to ways of dealing with emerging markets, facilities needs, and even basic human resource requirements. But the winds of change that have reshaped the culture of corporate America are surely blowing through the hallways of American schools too.

Governance can be characterized by what it takes care of and what it leaves to chance. The governance of big-city school systems takes care of many things: school board members' prerogatives as senior public officials, the salaries and job rights of teachers, and voters' belief that, even if things are not going well now, something is being done and the situation promises to get better.

Table 2-1 summarizes this entire book. It outlines the critique of public education governance that has emerged from Brookings work on big-city school systems. And it suggests institutional remedies that this book develops in detail.

In table 2-1, the column on the left defines, broadly speaking, what existing governance arrangements guarantee. For all the criticisms of urban public schools, most of them are competent at many routine tasks.[3] Every payday, millions of employees get a paycheck that is correct down to the last penny and the last cent taken out for health care and other benefits. Each morning of the school year, millions of students are picked up at the right time and dropped off at the correct school in time for classes to begin. Then they are delivered home to the right house in the afternoon. Most big-city school systems operate not just the largest transportation system in town, but also the biggest chain of restaurants—routinely feeding breakfast, lunch, snacks, and even dinner to tens of thousands of children, five days a week.[4]

Table 2-1. *New Institutions to Correct Failures of Governance*

Ensured	Desired but not guaranteed	Institutional remedies
Board prerogatives and political objectives	Environment that allows schools to focus on teaching	Civic oversight capacity
Financial commitments to employees and contractors	Adaptive use of funds	
Teachers' placements and working conditions	School effectiveness	
Programs demanded by organized groups	Options for children whom current schools do not serve well	School incubator
Hiring and keeping the numbers of teachers and administrators needed to staff the schools	Hiring and nurturing the best possible teachers and administrators	Human resource development institutions
Providing new initiatives to create senses of momentum and hope	Effective strategies that— Track data on results Sustain action Start corrective action	Data and analysis capacity
Facilities for existing schools and programs	Facilities for new schools and programs	Real estate trust

So the left-hand column in table 2-1 delineates several areas in which current governance arrangements ensure that adults' concerns for themselves are addressed. Board members can rest easy that their prerogatives as board members and their political imperatives will be acknowledged and probably respected. Financial commitments to employees and contractors will be met. The placement of teachers, and their seniority rights to select the schools in which they will work, is always a prime consideration, frequently operating under union agreements about working conditions and rights to grieve. Organized groups representing athletics, the gifted and talented, local auto body shops, music stores, and children with disabilities are guaranteed a respectful hearing; although they may not always obtain what they want, no one will question their right to seek it.

Interestingly, although everyone acknowledges the importance of good teachers and administrators, it is not quality that is ensured but quantity. Faced with overcrowded classrooms or burgeoning enrollment, district administrators sometimes settle for putting unqualified teachers in front of students. A classroom without a teacher is a much bigger headache than a classroom with an unqualified teacher. This explains why more than one-quarter of all American high school science teachers (and nearly one-third of those in science) are teaching "out of field," the euphemism used to disguise the reality that many teachers are unqualified.[5]

Because any city resident paying even minimal attention to local schools is distressed by their performance, current governance arrangements also provide for new initiatives that offer a sense of hope and optimism that things will get better. But as Frederick M. Hess has written, most of these reform initiatives are ephemeral in nature, more sound than fury, developed to legitimate the status quo by promising citizens that something is being done, even if that something amounts to recycling initiatives that failed earlier, or elsewhere.[6] Finally, although new schools often die for the lack of an available facility, the bonding and school construction process provides a tried-and-true means of obtaining public funds to refurbish existing facilities.

Important educational objectives that are pursued, but often left to chance, are equally interesting. These desirable outcomes are outlined in the middle column of table 2-1. Whether or not schools operate in an environment that permits principals and teachers to concentrate on teaching and learning is never a sure thing. While commitments to employees and contractors will always be met, the school's freedom to use funds adaptively rarely is. Schools' freedom to select staff, set boundaries, make strategic use of funds, allocate time, and develop strong internal cultures is left to chance. Options for children who are not succeeding in current schools receive little attention. While there are all kinds of special services, the unspoken belief is that the onus for fitting in falls on the student's shoulders. Parents of children with severe disabilities may challenge this belief successfully and demand special placement for their offspring, but most parents do not attempt to obtain individualized treatment. Although districts make good faith efforts to hire good teachers, no one is under any illusion that they hire the best or even set out to find them.

So too, although initiating plausible solutions to the most visible problems is essential, little is done to track data on results, sustain these new efforts, or make sure that new initiatives work as intended or are recalibrated in light of early experience. Similarly, though there is an imperative to make sure existing schools have facilities, there is no imperative to make room for new schools, even ones with promising approaches to instruction. The result is a shallow promise to the general public. Citizens who seek publicly funded alternative or charter schools are often assured they can have them. But a sort of Catch-22 is called into play—public funds can be used to support services in these schools, but no funds are available to provide a facility in which to house the new school. Even charter school operators, who are promised equal public spending for their students on a per pupil basis, find they have to finance their facility from these funds.

New Institutional Remedies

The information in the right-hand column of table 2-1 provides the structure for this book. It identifies six new institutions and capabilities designed to make sure that important educational outcomes are not left to chance but receive sustained attention—either in the urban district itself or outside it.

The first thing that is required is greater civic capacity to ensure that reform goes beyond what Hess has called "spinning wheels" and "policy churn" and attains some critical, sustained mass demonstrating genuine promise of results. School boards, district administrators, teachers, and unions can try to improve schools, but going much beyond symbolic action is often blocked by the internal dynamics of the district, politics, and the agreements that have been negotiated among them over the years. A civic oversight capacity, some group that is external to the board and the school system itself, is essential to oversee the implementation of reform. Chapter 3 describes such a capacity and describes how it might operate.

Next, public education desperately needs the capacity to develop, nurture, and start new kinds of schools. Chapters 4 and 5 address this challenge. Statewide policies and preferences of the general public have forced local schools to seek "super majorities" before incurring capital outlays. So a new bond referendum to build or rehabilitate school buildings typically requires support from 60 percent or more of those voting on the measure. This requirement has created all kinds of problems for school leaders. It has set institutional blinders on local districts, encouraging them to think that the only way to finance a new school is through the bonding process. But every other unit of government, from the local to the federal levels, thinks nothing of maintaining a flexible portfolio of capital assets, owning some and leasing and renting others as needed. Chapter 4, developed by Michael DeArmond, explores some innovative ways to pay for and manage school facilities.

Another problem created by existing conventions for financing capital outlays is that most school districts are dragged kicking and screaming into creating new schools. The process of gaining a super majority is fraught with political danger and the potential for district personnel to be subjected to unpleasant attacks and even personal abuse. Indeed, the process is so perilous to budding administrative careers that district managers resist creating new schools. They prefer to make existing schools larger with the addition of portable classrooms. But, as the Bill and Melinda Gates Foundation and others are recognizing, there are many educational benefits to smaller and more intimate schools. Starting such schools, however, is rarely easy. Difficulties with school start-up have stimulated creation of *school incubators* in a few localities. Abigail Winger's chapter 5 explores what a school incubator might look like in a large urban district.

Chapters 6 and 7 take up one of the pressing issues in school districts and state capitols across the United States—how to get the best possible teachers and leaders into the schools. In chapter 6, Sarah Brooks and Paul Hill suggest establishing a regional human resource clearinghouse, one that serves all schools in a locality but is not a part of any one school district. It would help schools find people with rare as well as common skills and encourage a two-way flow of professionals between teaching and other careers. In chapter 7, Hill and Brooks suggest how the same kind of institution could recruit and promote the career development of school leaders.

Next, although big-city schools have had good school system evaluation offices, in the long run, no district is likely to be able to invest enough in these functions to maintain them effectively. And in truth the independence of these offices can never be guaranteed against pressure from the central system to provide analyses that support district management, either by providing a flow of positive findings or working on the latest district crisis. Chicago is one of a few large districts that can draw on an independently funded and scrupulously neutral capacity for data and analysis. Marguerite Roza's chapter 8 explores what such a capacity can mean for urban districts and suggests how it could be established and financed.

Education in the United States has looked for external validation of school quality through the regional accreditation process. This system relies on extensive school self-studies, backed up by teams of observers who spend three to five days on site validating the self-study and making recommendations for improvement. More recently, encouraged by statutes such as the No Child Left Behind legislation, student assessment data have become the focus of institutional accountability. There is also some interest in adopting something similar to the English model of school inspectors. In chapter 9, James Harvey explores the possibilities of the inspectorate approach.

Finally, the coeditors, Hill and Harvey, pull these disparate elements together and show what needed institutions will cost, all in chapter 10. They argue that local districts are unlikely to invest in these institutions and strategies and call on a new philanthropic "third way" that invests in these institutions as a way to avoid the dilemma of investing in failure or ignoring entirely the needs of urban schools.

Notes

1. See, for example, Ronald Brownstein, "Federal Funds Should Educate, Not Just Employ," *Los Angeles Times*, February 4, 2002.

2. Howard L. Fuller, George A. Mitchell, and Michael E. Hartmann, *The Milwaukee Public Schools' Teacher Union Contract: Its History, Content, and Impact on Education* (Milwaukee: Institute for the Transformation of Learning, Marquette University, 1997).

3. For this insight and the examples that follow, we are indebted to Martin Haberman and a presentation he made at the Missouri Superintendents Forum in October 2001. See *Finding (and Keeping) Great Teachers*, Highlights of the Missouri Superintendents Forum, 2001 (Kansas City: Ewing Marion Kauffman Foundation, 2002).

4. One sign of how well most systems perform these and related functions can be read in the public outrage of what happens when important district systems collapse. New Orleans citizens were angered to hear in 1998 that payroll errors had produced glitches in paychecks for more than a year and had even left about 1,000 employees without a paycheck during a one-week period. Similar problems continue to this day. See State of Louisiana Legislative Auditor, *Investigative Audit Report* (New Orleans School Board, May 23, 2002). See also Rob Nelson, "School Paycheck Problems Return, New Orleans," *Times Picayune*, June 15, 2004 (www.nola.com [June 23, 2004]). In Washington, D.C., a city that had notoriously tolerated low performance among students and teachers for decades, an incumbent superintendent was unceremoniously shown the door for mismanagement in the late 1990s. The reasons? Schools could not open on time in the fall for two years in a row because of potentially dangerous roofs. Meanwhile, after newspaper audits indicated the district's payroll system was issuing paychecks to nonexistent, possibly deceased, people, the superintendent acknowledged in public that it was impossible to say how many employees the district had. For a summary of many of these developments, see Valerie Strauss and Sari

Horowitz, "D.C. Schools: A System in Crisis," *Washington Post*, February 17, 1997, p. A1.

5. "Out-of-Field Teaching," National Center for Education Statistics (http://nces.ed.gov/ssbr/pages/field.asp [June 23, 2004]).

6. Frederick M. Hess, *Spinning Wheels: The Politics of Urban School Reform* (Brookings, 1998) p. 5.

THREE *New Capacity for*
Civic Oversight

PAUL T. HILL

LARGE PUBLIC SCHOOL districts are "in" the com-
munity but only rarely are they "of" it. Their strength is also their weak-
ness: somehow urban schools stand apart from the other major political
and economic forces driving their cities. This independence, something
that is supported by the tenure and civil-service status enjoyed by their
employees, is intended to buffer them from partisan politics. Their bonding authority provides local educators with formidable local clout and
autonomy in the face of the roller coaster of municipal finance. The independence of local school boards is thought to protect schools from what
might be intolerable meddling from local politicians. On balance, there is
a lot to justify this traditional deference to the autonomy of the local school
system.

Yet this isolation comes with significant costs. Schools, shielded from
the hurly-burly of local politics, are often isolated from many important
political currents running through the community. Has a major local employer shut the doors? That is a concern, but otherwise of little significance to a school board that has been planning a bond issue for a year or
more. Districts are even insulated from the realities of competition for
market share that drive so many other institutions. School districts can
lose student population for years, but as long as the loss of students is no
faster than the rate of teachers' retirement, nobody in the district sees a
serious problem. That is why school districts in Seattle and Dayton continued largely with business as usual during a thirty-year period when
their student populations dropped by 50 percent or more.

Isolation from external pressures makes school districts highly attentive to their internal politics. Superintendents, central offices, teachers unions, and school boards presumably want to improve schools, but their disagreements lead to deadlock. District leaders might want schools to take the initiative in tailoring instruction to students' needs, but they can not change use-of-time regulations, teacher-work rules, or strictures on the use of funds. Districts can try to improve their teaching forces by investing in in-service training, but they cannot weed out mediocre teachers or try hiring teachers with different qualifications.[1] Nor can they with any regularity close failed schools or create alternatives for children who have been trapped in such schools.

Effective reform strategies, strong and long lasting enough to transform the educational opportunities of thousands of children in big-city schools, are possible. But they do not come easily or without conflict. They require fundamental changes of three kinds. First, performance incentives—so that it matters a great deal to principals and teachers whether the children in their care learn. Next, investments in new capacity—so that schools can strengthen their faculties (through training and recruitment) and improve their methods and materials. Finally, schools need freedom of action, so that teachers and principals can use their expertise on behalf of students.[2]

Effective reform strategies generate opposition often leading to turnover in superintendents, school boards, and union leaders; they must be sustained even when leaders are replaced. In fact, a reform strategy that does not explicitly provide for leadership turnover amounts to little more than a false promise to the general public.

Too often, particularly when school boards seek a new superintendent, the sense is that the district needs better leadership and, ideally, a leader with a plan. But in fact, what the community really should possess is a mission and strategy that new leaders inherit—not leaders with recycled ideas attractively decorated in new colors. Understanding the strategy, and support for its continuation, must be lodged somewhere more stable and longer lasting than any organ of the school district. Superintendents turn over frequently. So too do school boards. The teachers union is long lasting, but, as only one party with specific interests in school reform, it cannot be allowed to dominate policy.

A Civic Leadership Group

What is the alternative? If the cycle-time of board and superintendent turnover is shorter than the cycle of reform implementation, reform strategies will always be abandoned before they can bear fruit. Though boards and superintendents can seize the agenda for a time, their inevitable departure means that other more stable entities, particularly the teachers union and permanent central office staff, are most likely to get what they want in the long run.

Mayors might provide the strategic leadership and implementation guidance needed to stabilize an education reform strategy, but they too are subject to defeat and distraction. Politically stable cities like Chicago and Boston might sustain a school reform strategy under mayoral leadership, but in most places the mayor's chair is too unsteady.

Another option, and the one we think most promising, is the kind of civic leadership group that guides big cities through major transitions. These are groups, like the Chicago Civic Committee and the Cincinnati Business Committee, that normally organize applications for the Olympics or mount campaigns to support investments to transform the city's economic infrastructure. Traditionally, mayors and business leaders have dominated such groups, but these leadership entities now, quite properly, include minority, community, and religious leaders.

Such groups can help greatly to define and sustain reform strategy. Besides preserving the flame of the city's educational vision, these groups can operate as buffers between the schools and the community, interpreting the district to the larger community and the community's crosscurrents to the district.

Civic leadership groups are unelected and have no formal powers. They are volunteer organizations led and supported by people who think government alone is unlikely to address the long-term threats to the city's well-being, or to press civic initiatives whose costs are felt in the short term and whose benefits appear only over time. Across the nation, almost every major city can draw on a coalition of powerful local interests to advance the city's well-being. Chicago's Civic Committee, for example, transformed the downtown and waterfront. Pittsburgh's Allegheny Conference helped clean up air pollution in the city, revitalized downtown, and helped legendary school superintendent Richard Wallace transform the schools in the 1980s. Cincinnati's Business Committee led a levy campaign for adequate school funding and uses its clout in the state capital to win the school system relief from burdensome regulations. In Washington, D.C., the Board of Trade has employed its mandate to improve the business climate to lobby for District home rule, a state-of-the-art subway system, and improvements in city schools.

Although the makeup of each of these groups differs modestly, the most effective seem to include leaders from several different communities: the political establishment, business community, and foundation and art worlds.

Such groups could work effectively in education. As in other areas they would work to set the agenda for elected officials and act as watchdogs on strategy implementation. They would not, however, assume governmental power themselves. Their only power would be to define a strategy and act as a powerful interest group to advocate for adoption and execution. In education, a civic leadership group could take on several critical tasks. They could mobilize electoral support for a reform design, help strategies for reform survive the turnover of superintendents, oppose proposals that distract from reform, and press for termination of old arrangements. The groups could also arrange needed regulatory relief and financial support from the state capitol, track progress and work on reversing failure, and build a grassroots constituency for reform among parents.

Winning Elections

Community leaders must understand that school board elections are the forums in which entire reform initiatives can be sustained or lost. Nothing can protect a reform against a newly elected school board that claims a mandate to decimate the reform strategy or fire a superintendent. School boards are not good forums for creating integrated strategy, but they are excellent platforms from which reform initiatives and their leaders can be destroyed.

A civic reform oversight group cannot guarantee election results or prevent a well-mobilized majority from having its way. But it can develop an election strategy, provide public information, make sure that good candidates are fielded, and manage voter turnout initiatives, all indispensable parts of reform implementation.

Surviving Superintendent Succession

Reviewing the history of reform in any major urban area is a sobering experience. In cities such as Kansas City (Missouri), Hartford, and Dallas, the schools have been lost for close to a decade or more, while turnover among superintendents has been constant. Even in cities where superintendents change less frequently, successive reform efforts are likely to resemble each fall television line-up. Just as the television networks annually announce a predictable blend of high drama, low comedy, and sports as though it were new, so too do urban districts regularly offer up a portfolio of reading, the basic skills, and discipline strategies as though these things had never been thought of before.

The typical big-city superintendent's two-and-one-half-year tenure is far too short to create and institutionalize a reform strategy. Faced with the likelihood of turnover of superintendents, leaders of a civic reform oversight group must make sure successive superintendents are hired to continue and build on the city's reform strategy, not reject and replace it.

In truth, a change in superintendents offers communities many opportunities to think about what they have been accomplishing. Ideally, turnover should be an opportunity for an honest look at what has been accomplished. Too frequently, of course, these occasions turn into finger-pointing and blame about what went wrong, instead of an open discussion about how things are going. But properly handled, these transitions offer the opportunity to amend strategy or improve implementation. A civic reform oversight group needs to pay close attention to the school board's preparations to hire a new superintendent and use its moral authority—and the mayor's influence—to make sure that the premises on which new superintendents are hired reaffirm the city's commitment to its basic reform strategy.

Opposing Distracting Proposals and Terminating Old Arrangements

The civic reform oversight group can demonstrate a plan's staying power in two ways. First, the group can resist new policies and mandates that are not demonstrably part of the reform plan. Second, it can identify rules, administrative structures, and uses of funds that are not consistent with the reform plan and should be terminated. The first part of this prescription requires self-discipline. Civic leaders cannot push for every new "silver bullet" they hear about at national conferences or from their friends. The standard for judgment is easy: if a new idea does not solve a problem for which city leaders were openly seeking a solution, it should not be added to the mix.

The second part of the prescription may be even more important. In most cities, successive efforts to improve the schools have left behind geological layers of half-implemented reforms. Each of these initiatives lasted long enough to leave some residue of habit, policy, or staff members committed to it. If a city's reform initiative is to succeed, leaders must persuade teachers and principals that it is here to stay.

Civic leadership groups must do something that is rarely attempted in school administration: they must decide what the school system will no longer do. Previous reform efforts will have created special central office structures, methods of allocating teachers and other resources to schools, and collective bargaining provisions that prevent schools from changing. If these underlying structures are not terminated, they will tear any new reform plan to pieces. Only a group as powerful and politically independent as the civic reform oversight group can pursue the task of termination relentlessly enough to succeed.

Arranging Regulatory Relief and State Support

A civic reform oversight group can help promote flexible use of funds provided by the state or passed through the state from the federal government. Sometimes, all that is required is that someone asks for help. Leaders of a civic reform oversight group do not have to accept the first thing they hear about what is permissible and what cannot be done. They can and should be the community's leading edge in seeking advice and cooperation from high-level state and federal officials, including their state's governor and the U.S. secretary of education.

A civic reform oversight group speaking for a major city should have little difficulty successfully advocating for needed changes. Serious reform strategies will need more than waivers and accommodations from the state and federal government. They will need permanent changes in laws on how schools are funded, how money is used, and how teachers are hired. Foundation heads and business CEOs have direct access to the governor and senior legislators and can plead their locality's case effectively. They have far more leverage in the state capital than any school superintendent, and they can deal directly with top government leaders, over the heads of state education agency officials. Procter and Gamble's successful advocacy for Cincinnati school reform is exemplary.

Tracking Failures and Acting to Fix Problems

Reform strategies can take many years to have desired effects on student learning. Community leaders who "wind it up and forget it" will eventually learn that important parts of the reform strategy never happened or happened in ways other than originally designed. The only way to prevent unpleasant surprises of implementation failure is to create systems of "leading indicators." These tell reform leaders whether key implementation tasks have been done as expected and whether school staff and students are responding in the ways expected. For example, oversight of a reform strategy whose first step is to allocate all funds to schools on a per pupil basis should make clear whether money was distributed as intended. It might also verify whether school leaders had the freedom to spend these funds, and whether they used them in ways anticipated by the reform strategy. Positive results do not prove that the reform will work, but negative ones would almost certainly imply that the reform would not achieve the intended effects unless implementation is corrected.

Close oversight of reform implementation is rare in public education. In Chicago, the one city in which such oversight is routinely done, the superintendent and chief administrators often resent being told that plans are not fully implemented or that initiatives are not having the intended short-term effects. However, Chicago's reform oversight agency, the Chicago Consortium on School Research, has persisted despite hostile reactions from officials. The result, ironically, is to sustain the reform by reminding citizens what was promised and by ensuring that implementation failures are quickly addressed.

Reform leaders must be eager to get the facts and adjust implementation when things are not going according to plan. Though the people in charge of day-to-day reform implementation inevitably care about appearances, heads of foundations and business philanthropies should care only about results. They are therefore the right ones to establish and pay for oversight and adjustment of the reform.

Building a Parent Constituency

Though senior civic leaders are legitimate initiators of school reform, strategies cannot be sustained without grassroots support. In the end, everything depends on parents. If they understand the direction of reform and are confident that it is benefiting their children, no group is likely to oppose it effectively. Unfortunately, parents seldom have any concrete understanding of what is being done or why. Like teachers, poor and minority parents have seen superintendents and reform slogans come and go and understandably doubt the seriousness of any initiative. Uninformed parents are susceptible to manipulation by school system insiders who oppose the reform and claim, "Whatever these outsiders are doing, it will hurt your kids."

Parents need to know why a reform strategy is being initiated, how it is supposed to work, and how it will affect their children. They should also know what changes to expect in their schools and whom to call if they see that promised changes are not happening. Even when superintendents and board members support a reform strategy, school districts cannot be trusted to provide needed information about it. Permanent central office staff and union leaders may support the change, but they can just as easily create a flow of counterreform information, which the superintendent is powerless to stop. Even if district and union leaders support the new efforts, the rank and file may oppose them. In some states and communities (for example, Kentucky), major reform initiatives have had to be remodeled or justified anew because teachers, distressed by the direction of reform and its new demands, persuaded parents that the reforms were bad for their children. Perhaps not surprisingly, it turns out that most parents rely on their children's teachers for advice on whether to support or complain about changes in the school.

A civic reform oversight group must provide layman-friendly explanations of the reform and make sure parents are never surprised about how their children's schools will be affected. In every case, the group's goal should be to avoid having to mount defensive campaigns against rumors, by telling the story first and giving parents the proper framework for receiving information.

For parents, the most valuable information is about their choices among schools and instructional programs. School profiles, simple documents explaining options, and school choice fairs (where parents can meet teachers from many schools) are all central elements of an information strategy. The civic reform oversight group should organize and provide financial support for these functions, not wait for the school district to initiate them.

Conclusion

A civic reform oversight group is a political solution to a political problem. It does not create a new bureaucracy or make government decisionmaking more complex. All it does is create a capacity to make public a broader agenda than the special interest politics of groups that now dominate district decisionmaking. It also uses the political clout of a city's most influential residents on behalf of education, whether in raising funds, seeking relief from state regulation, or attracting talented administrators.

Such oversight groups have certain values: they want their city to grow, prosper, and remain an attractive place to live, and they believe in investment now for long-term benefits. Not everybody agrees those values should always come first—conflicts over whether dollars should go toward investment, or instead to current payments for teachers and existing programs, are inevitable.

By suggesting that such groups formulate and stabilize reform strategies, we do not think they will—or should—always prevail. There are other priorities, and civic oversight groups might try to defend strategies that need to be abandoned. However, without a civic oversight group there is little chance that a city can sustain a fundamental reform strategy long enough for it to work. Such a group makes sustained reform possible, not certain.

Notes

1. In Cincinnati and Rochester (N.Y.), union leaders were thwarted in their efforts to create strong programs of teacher assessment.

2. These three essential elements are laid out more fully in Paul T. Hill, Christine Campbell, and James Harvey, *It Takes a City: Getting Serious about Urban School Reform* (Brookings, 2000).

FOUR

Getting out of the Facilities Business

MICHAEL DeARMOND

IN MARCH 2002, superintendent John Martin from Grandview, Missouri, found his class at Harvard's John F. Kennedy School of Government interrupted by an emergency phone call from his district. The unstable gable wall of a fifty-year-old school was moving more rapidly than anyone had anticipated, and his worried administrators wanted to know whether or not they should close the school for their students' protection. A similar dilemma had faced Washington, D.C. Superintendent Franklin Smith several years earlier, and it had cost him his job. Faced with a court decision requiring him to certify that his schools met fire codes, Smith could not open several schools on time for two years in a row. He was eventually fired.[1] Smith's successor, former army general Julius Becton, vowed to turn things around. But after less than a year on the job, Becton found himself voting to close eighteen schools for code violations. After seventeen months as superintendent, he quit.[2]

Becton, Smith, and Martin are not alone. Providing suitable buildings is a huge challenge for superintendents and school districts across the country. Recent surveys show that one-quarter of the nation's districts have at least one entire building in "less than adequate condition" and that half of all schools have at least one "inadequate building feature" (for example, failing roofs, floors, foundations, or electrical systems).[3] One in four American public schools operates above capacity, and a full one-third use portable classrooms to accommodate the overflow. Los Angeles's schools are bursting at the seams; Detroit's remain run-down despite a $1.5 billion bond measure. The stories are legion.

Yet overcrowding and disrepair are not the complete story. New and innovative schools have trouble just getting *access* to the buildings they need. High costs, inadequate capital funding, and political opposition to using district-owned space can make it hard for charter schools to find the buildings they need. Small schools fight an uphill battle in a world where districts continue to build high schools to hold 1,600 students in classrooms with thirty desks each. So beyond the obvious damage done by overcrowded classrooms and broken windows, problems with facilities can frustrate reform. In either case, the effect is similar: a district's current stock of buildings limits how teachers can teach and how children can learn.

These problems are not easy to address. Superintendents and school boards face real challenges when it comes to providing quality buildings for both existing and new types of schools—especially when they see new ones as a key part of long-lasting reform. At the same time, we should recognize that school districts do not have to be the sole actors working to meet these challenges. This chapter outlines an idea for a new institution for governing school facilities called a Public School Real Estate Trust. The idea's bottom line is to uncouple the property management function from school district central offices. The purpose is to improve the management of district assets and ensure that facilities do not constrain the educational opportunities a district can offer its children. While a Trust could open up alternative methods of financing school buildings, it is important to recognize that this is not a solution to the difficult problem of facilities funding; and although a Trust could, and indeed should, support school reform, it is not a stand-alone strategy. Its role and effect would depend on a district's broader strategy for reform.

Rationale for the Trust

Historically, local school districts have been entirely responsible for funding and managing school buildings. Although districts generally still own and manage their buildings, today most states (about three-fifths) use a combination of state and local funding for school buildings.[4] Whatever the details of that funding combination—it can range from full state funding to state loans and flat grants—school districts tend to respond narrowly to questions about facilities supply: districts ask voters if the district can borrow money to construct schools that the district will own and manage.

This approach does not necessarily cause problems, but when it is the only option, its limits are clear. In some districts, getting voter approval to borrow money can be difficult, if not impossible, often requiring a super majority vote of 60 percent. Municipal debt obligations can constrain budgets. Depending on the market and a district's bond rating, the actual cost of borrowing money can also be high. Other less visible costs include fees from banks, brokers, bond syndicates, and attorneys. Finally, communities with large tax bases can raise money more easily than those with few revenue resources.[5]

So far, nothing about these problems necessarily calls for a new institution to manage school real estate. Indeed, a district could try to address funding problems by pursuing alternative financing arrangements that avoid the drawbacks of bond elections and debt financing (for example, using certificates of participation).[6] It might try to reduce capital costs by sharing a building or recreational space with another public agency (for example, parks and recreation departments, health clinics, day care) or a compatible private organization (for example, the YMCA). It might even look for a third party to design, finance, and build a school for lease. In fact, small numbers of districts across the country are already trying these and other new approaches to meet their needs for facilities. The rationale for a new institution, then, does not necessarily come from the limitations associated with how districts currently pay for buildings. Instead, the rationale comes from the problems connected with district management and ownership of school buildings.

District Management and Ownership

Managing school buildings is a big task. It involves determining schools' needs, developing improvement programs, updating facilities plans, analyzing demographics and enrollment data, supervising designs, managing construction, and much more. In most districts, central office employees do all of this work. To be sure, keeping facilities management in-house has its advantages. It allows districts to closely control the location and quality of their buildings, and it internalizes transactions that might require complex legal agreements if they involved outsiders. And yet, despite these advantages, the liabilities of in-house facilities management can cause problems for both existing schools and, especially, new ones. Three problems stand out: opportunity costs, capacity and flexibility, and investment incentive.

Opportunity Costs

Most people can think of urban high schools that sit on prime city real estate. District ownership of these buildings (like ownership of anything) includes large *opportunity costs* that school boards and superintendents may not fully appreciate.[7] When a district owns a school building, it is in effect sacrificing the alternative of selling or leasing that building at market value. This in no way suggests that districts should sell off or lease out valuable properties just because there is money to be made; it simply suggests that in some cases they might. As San Diego superintendent Alan Bersin put it in a January 2004 interview with one of the editors of this volume, inefficient use of real estate is not instructionally neutral: it wastes money that could otherwise be used for instruction. District officials can discern opportunity costs by asking questions such as, How much is district real estate really worth? If we sold an asset and then leased it back, could we raise extra money to spend on educational programs? What are the potential benefits and liabilities of disposing of capital assets to finance current operations? Could we use a mixed-use agreement to squeeze out some of the market value of our properties? Do we need all of the space we own? How could our assets provide better long-term return for the district? Too often, school officials do not ask these tough questions. This limitation is partly because of the second problem connected with district ownership and management.

Capacity and Flexibility

Educators are trained to be educators, not real estate developers or investors. And yet, as their careers advance, some educators may find themselves making the transition to real estate manager, whether or not they have the right expertise or training. With in-house facilities management, districts can struggle to get the technical talent they need to ask creative questions about their assets and to pursue new approaches to school buildings that address changing circumstances. As Oklahoma City School Board member Ron Bogle says, "Our educators are trained to be educators, and they may not necessarily have the skills to deal with really large, complex construction projects. We ought to take advantage of those in our community who have that ability."[8]

The second part of this problem is inflexibility. Districts can be slow to respond to new and different ways of doing things thanks to, among other things, existing rules and organizational culture. In New York City, for example, a lack of coordination between the school system's leasing, legal, and renovation departments delayed the opening of several small schools in the 1990s. Only one opened as originally planned, two had to move at least three times in the first year, two had to move once more during the first school year, and two were located in spaces that might not remain theirs beyond the first year.[9] At best, new schools can expect support through a policy of exception and waiver; at worst, they can be punished for not fitting the mold. In the end, standard approaches to facilities management can be reasonable solutions for standard school buildings. But when they are the exclusive solution, they create problems for new schools and innovative ideas, forming a major obstacle to what James Harvey and Paul T. Hill call "powerful and long-lasting reform."[10]

Investment Incentive

Finally, when school facilities are in-house, the deck is stacked against investing in and maintaining them. School board members, like other public officials facing elections, have an incentive to focus on the here and now instead of their district's long-term capital investment needs. David Weimer and Aiden Vining explain this dilemma: "Consider a representative who must stand for reelection in, say, two years. Because his constituency does not fully monitor his behavior, he faces the problem of convincing the electorate that his actions have contributed to their well being. He will undoubtedly realize that it will be easier to claim credit for effects that have actually occurred than for ones expected to occur in the future."[11]

A shortened time horizon can lead officials to minimize future costs and benefits and instead favor projects with short-run benefits. The result is underinvestment in capital infrastructure and facilities.[12]

Taken together, problems with facilities financing and governance can lead to run-down buildings for existing schools and inadequate space for new ones. As already mentioned, districts can consider alternative financial arrangements like purchase-lease agreements where a developer builds and leases a facility to a district, or public-private partnerships for shared facilities use, or new school designs that are more flexible and more connected to the people and purposes they serve.[13]

On a broader scale, politicians have called for increased state or regional facilities funding, think tanks have proposed infrastructure banks capitalized by the federal government to help districts get access to capital, and charter school advocates have called for per pupil capital funding, lease aid, or laws that would allow charter schools to issue tax exempt bonds. These proposals have real merits. And yet, in some ways, they offer partial solutions. Some infuse the current system with more funding but leave the fundamentals of facilities governance intact and do little to help charters, small schools, contract schools, or other innovations. Others fund a few alternatives at the margin—charters or a single school—but do little to address changes in the system at large or to help current schools stuck in failing buildings. Many do little to enhance district capacity or flexibility. If a district sees quality facilities for both existing schools and new kinds of schools as a key for long-lasting reform, it may want to consider a bolder idea: getting out of the real estate business.

A New Institution: The Public Schools Real Estate Trust

In *It Takes a City*, Paul T. Hill, Christine Campbell, and James Harvey proposed an idea for uncoupling the property management function from district central services. They called for a new institution, a Public Schools Real Estate Trust, which would become the owner of all public school buildings.[14] The Trust would maintain a portfolio of buildings for all public schools; it would sell, build, or lease new buildings as needed to meet the district's needs. This new organization, by virtue of its clear mission, managerial independence, and flexibility, would, in theory, help ensure that all publicly funded schools have access to quality buildings. It would help extend a district's capacity by marshaling new talent and resources. It would make investments to maintain the long-term functional and financial value of the district's facilities. It would serve all public schools, not just traditional ones. These are high hopes that cannot be fully addressed by this brief treatment. Still, by presenting some broad thoughts about how a school district might create a Trust, how a Trust might operate, and what challenges it might raise for school officials, this chapter urges school leaders to think creatively about supplying facilities as a way to improve educational opportunities of children.

The only school district that has created a Trust, to my knowledge, is Portland Public Schools in Portland, Oregon. In 2001, a special task force appointed by the school board concluded that Portland had spent significantly more per student on operations and maintenance than the state average. Part of the problem was that the district had 30 percent *more* building space per student than other districts, even though the district's per square foot maintenance and operations cost was lower. Portland's buildings were also older than the state average and so required more maintenance. Finally, the district was providing space to several community partners at rates below the cost to the district.

In response to the task force's findings and recommendations, the district commissioned a local nonprofit to develop a Long Range Facilities

Plan for the district. Among its proposals, the Long Range Facilities Plan laid out the rationale for creating the Portland Schools Real Estate Trust. The school board established the Trust in early 2002. At the time, the Trust was introduced mainly as a way to help the district lease, sell, or redevelop its "surplus" properties. Although Portland's Trust failed to meet Hill, Campbell, and Harvey's lofty expectations about reforming facilities policy, Portland's experience of grappling with the mission, structure, leadership, and operations of a Trust offers some practical ideas for how a district might start and operate a semiautonomous Trust.[15]

Mission

The Trust's mission might be as broad as ensuring that all public schools have timely access to quality space, as noted in *It Takes a City*, but it could just as easily have a narrower purpose: selling off surplus property to realize a good return for the district and improve property management practices.[16] Brian Scott, one of the founders of Portland's Trust, suggests that one of the reasons Portland's Trust failed to gain traction in its first year of operation was that people had different ideas about its role. Some saw the Trust as simply the district's agent in real estate deals; others had a broader vision of the Trust acting as the manager of all of the district's properties, including its active schools. Despite the fact that district leaders seemed to embrace the idea of the Trust's preeminence in facilities management when it was established in early 2002, a year later the Trust had yet to move beyond providing expert real estate advice to the district on particular properties. As we discuss later, part of the problem was that just as the Trust was launched, a host of political and budgetary problems drew the district's attention elsewhere.

If a district envisions a Trust as its real estate expert, the Trust's work is fairly straightforward and may be limited to giving advice and negotiating property deals on surplus real estate. But if a district intends to have the Trust manage *all* of its buildings to better support reform, complicated management and policy issues arise about who is using which district spaces, under what conditions, and for how long; the coordination of instructional and facilities management; and the stewardship of historic civic buildings and the connections between school facilities and urban development.

Structure

Portland's experience suggests that decisions about how to structure the Trust include weighing some trade-offs between the Trust's independence and its accountability to the district. Portland chose to structure its Trust as a single-member independent nonprofit 501(c)(3) corporation, of which the school district is the sole member. This move created an independent legal entity that was ultimately accountable to the district. Two factors drove Portland's decision. First, the district wanted to maintain a measure of control over the Trust to ensure that the school board could carry out its fiduciary duty to the public. Under Portland's structure, the school board has the authority to dissolve the Trust's board. If, by contrast, the Trust were a nonprofit with *no members*, the Trust board would be self-perpetuating, and the district would have far less control over it. Portland thought that without a veto—that is, the power to dissolve the Trust's board—the district's ability to ensure that the public interest was represented would be too limited.

Second, Portland wanted a structure that would protect the liability of the Trust's board. This caution was in part to make positions on the Trust's board more attractive to the caliber of volunteers the district hoped would serve on it. If Portland had created the Trust as a true *trustee* with the district as *beneficiary*, the members of the Trust board would have been held to strict fiduciary duty requirements for acting in the district's best interest and would have been personally exposed to liability. Under a nonprofit structure, the Trust's board members are held to the less strict Business Judgment Rule and are protected from personal liability as long as they act in good faith with due care.

Leadership

Assuming that the Trust's mission and legal status are clear, a district would then be responsible for appointing the Trust's board of directors— that is, it must decide who will run the Trust. Portland designed the Trust's board to be self-nominating (with confirmation by the district) to give it the independence to select board members whose skills fit the Trust's needs. A district could also decide to name the Trust's board directly. Regardless of who makes the decision, Portland's experience raises several issues related to the Trust's leadership.

Because one of the Trust's main purposes is to bring new expertise to bear on managing the district's assets, the board of directors should include community leaders with expertise in real estate investment, development, management, and sales, as well as experience with public agencies and community groups. Having real estate expertise *and* political savvy are important. According to Scott, Portland's Trust floundered partly because its board of directors, despite having a great deal of clout in real estate circles, was not well versed in the politics of public sector operations, especially the politics of the school district.

For political and practical reasons, the Trust should make it clear to the public that its board of directors will work solely with the district's interests in mind. In Portland, the Trust's board signed a no-personal-benefit agreement, promising not to benefit financially from any transactions involving school property. Given the complicated nature of real estate deals and the potential for people to question the Trust's motivation, Portland thought it was important to clarify that the Trust's board would act only in the public interest.

Finally, although a district might want to put a district official on the board of directors as an ex officio member (because doing so might give it a chance to monitor its interests), Portland decided that the Trust board would be better off without a district representative. The Trust's founders worried that putting a district official on the board would derail the Trust's work by entangling it in political and policy decisions that were better left to district leaders.

Operations

Reformers in Portland put the cost of the Trust at $350,000 to $400,000 a year, with a compensation package for the executive director in the range of $200,000. In practice, half of the Trust's budget was to be covered by the district, and the Trust's board was to raise the remainder from private sources. Once the district established the Trust and appointed a board of directors (who subsequently hired an executive director), it needed to draw up a legal document to describe the terms of its relationship to the Trust. Using Portland's *Property Disposition Assistance Agreement* as a guide, such a contract should cover:

—The Trust's mission and purpose; how long the agreement will last and how it can be terminated (for example, three to five years); and the methods by which the district can deed property to the Trust (for example, a bargain and sale deed).

—The Trust's goals and responsibilities, including broad items like ensuring all schools have the space they need and specific activities such as conducting appropriate studies and analyses, negotiating with prospective parties and partners, retaining brokers, and other actions).

—The district's specific responsibilities, including funding obligations and obligations such as signing applications for land use approvals advocated by the Trust.

—The relationship among schools, the district, and the Trust (for example, individual schools might have direct contact with the Trust for space arrangements, they might have zero-rent leases with the Trust, or they might access its resources indirectly through the district. This is one of the most difficult parts of the idea to work out and in the end depends on how comprehensive the Trust's responsibilities are).

—Financial management and accountability, including details such as the timing, method, and amount of payments between the Trust and the district and how to account for them.

—The district's plan for monitoring performance, which could include performance indicators and reporting and access to information requirements.

—Consequences for performance, which could range from financial bonuses for the executive director to increased scrutiny and reporting by the Trust.[17]

Once a district has drawn up a contract outlining its relationship with the Trust, the Trust would, in essence, become the exclusive agent handling district properties and real estate. The Trust could, depending on its mission, pursue various approaches to managing district property and providing space to schools. At a basic level, a Trust could help a district understand the full value of its assets. In Portland, for example, the Trust identified between fifty and one hundred acres of district land that offered the potential for many development opportunities without disrupting recreational fields. These properties were estimated to represent a little more than $100 million in opportunity costs for the district, when potential sales receipts, property tax revenues, and the value of increased enrollment from new housing units were added together.

A more active Trust might help arrange a deal to share a building or recreational space to reduce capital costs, help reduce redundant community facilities (theaters, swimming pools, playing fields), strengthen ties between schools and the community, and improve the coordination of social services for children and families. Of course officials would have to weigh the difficulties of joint occupancy: intricate coordination, complex funding, the loss of total district control over facilities, and potential liability issues.

Alternatively, the Trust could look for a third party to design, finance, and build one or more schools for lease rather than have the district build and own schools. Depending on the project, the Trust could sign on with a variety of lease agreements: an operating or true lease (simply paying rent); a capital lease (a purchase-to-own agreement); a sale-lease-back (selling an asset and leasing it back so the district gets cash and the buyer gets the tax advantages of asset ownership). These arrangements would allow a district to bypass debt limits and the need for voter approval and possibly give the district access to innovative financing and cost-saving techniques it otherwise would not have (for example, revenue bonds, certificates of participation, mortgages, or commercial notes).[18] They would also give the district flexibility; the Trust could get out of a lease if it needed to.[19]

Beyond financing and ownership alternatives, the Trust could explore other opportunities to improve school buildings. Schools could incorporate community cultural and social activities, youth programs, and recreation activities by expanding their hours of use. School and classroom designs could be made in light of new models of teaching and learning that call for student involvement and more active engagement in learning. At the same time, designs would allow adaptability for many uses (for example, spaces might accommodate various-sized learning groups—one hundred students, five groups of twenty, groups of twelve, or groups of four to six or one and two).[20]

Today, of course, school districts can enter into joint occupancy agreements. They can expand the use of their schools to include more community activities, and they can use innovative designs that support cooperative learning, project-based work, and interdisciplinary learning and team teaching. Some districts already do these things. But too often, they do not. This is not necessarily because districts resist them but because current governance arrangements often provide little capacity, flexibility, and investment that can move in this direction. The proponents of the Trust recognize that districts often do not have access to the expertise and resources needed to pursue long-lasting reform, which requires buildings for both existing and new schools. The Trust has the potential to ensure that a district's buildings facilitate its reform efforts, not frustrate them. With this promise, however, come new challenges.

Challenges

"Policymakers," notes Donald Kettl of the University of Wisconsin-Madison, "have often approached indirect government [that is, the reliance on third parties to deliver publicly funded goods and services] as a self-executing system."[21] Nothing, he continues, could be further from the truth. While uncoupling real estate management from school districts presents an opportunity for citizens, educators, and facilities planners to take a broader view of what constitutes an effective and appropriate learning environment, it would also, as Kettl suggests, place new demands on school officials.

For starters, school officials who engage with a Public Schools Real Estate Trust would need to be able to manage the contract between the two entities. District officials would have to specify their goals for facilities provision in the contract in a way that sets a clear direction for the Trust and allows them to monitor whether or not these things are working. Kettl nicely summarizes the complicated array of skills required when he writes, "The fundamental irony of privatization and its other third-party variants is that they require very, very strong public management to make them work well. Moreover, they require a skill set—writing and negotiating good written agreements, tracking the money, auditing results, and assessing performance—on which governments often place relatively little emphasis."[22]

This last point is particularly challenging. The needed managerial talents are in short supply. Districts and superintendents who want to engage third parties to help them solve public problems would do well to cultivate them. What is more, Kettl suggests a final, even more daunting, challenge. If an independent institution like the Trust is to work, "it requires strategic leadership by top officials in addition to tactical administration by managers."[23] That is, uncoupling the real estate function of a district for its own sake makes little sense; it has to be done in service of a strategic vision about what a system of schools should look like. Indeed, this may have been one of the central problems with Portland's effort. Portland's facilities reforms certainly had much going for them—a city with a history of progressive urban development policy, civic expertise that was mobilized around the facilities problem, and a school board that supported the idea. What it lacked, however, was a clearly defined vision for school facilities reform in support of a broader vision of reform. The challenge is to wed a vision for the future of facilities with institutional and governance arrangements that can deliver on it.

One of the attractions of creating new institutions to support school reform is the idea that, by virtue of their independence, they will be able to step out from under the weight of district politics. Portland's experience suggests that this is easier said than done. In Portland, a superintendent search, a budget crisis, and labor strife drew the district's attention away from the Trust during its early implementation. Some observers suggest that Portland's Trust had trouble weathering this storm in large part because it did not have its own base of support and power—such as the civic oversight capacity Hill describes in chapter 3—outside of the district. Ironically, reformers in Portland made a conscious decision to avoid creating the Trust as a political entity (this made sense given that Portland already has a powerful political counterweight to the district in the Portland Schools Foundation), but the Trust's lack of political strength left it on unsettled ground as the district's agenda became mired in budgetary and bureaucratic politics.

In the end, rethinking school facilities is a complicated business. It includes technical and organizational intricacies about property management and finance that are hard for any single educator to grasp. Indeed, it requires a team of people with specialized knowledge: educators, lawyers, accountants, politicians, real estate developers, architects, construction managers, and more, as part of both the Trust and the district. It requires thinking about the relationship between instruction programs and space. It requires thinking about how school facilities relate to a city's recreational spaces and development agenda; it is complicated by the symbolic and historical meaning that communities attach to their school buildings—the redevelopment of an old school site may make financial and educational sense and still make citizens and alumni angry. Above all, however, it requires superintendents and school boards who have the vision and courage to try something new.

Conclusion

The ways in which a district might rethink its facilities will depend on the challenges it faces and the resources it can marshal. When a district needs help on a single building or project (for example, a new high school or fixing up an old middle school), it may just consider new ways of paying for the building or designing it. When its leaders are serious about school reform and want to create a system of schools that offers more options for families and educators, they should, despite the real challenges involved, consider what they could gain by getting out of the nuts-and-bolts of the real estate business and focusing instead on the big picture.

Notes

1. See Michael Powell and Vernon Loeb, "For Reformers, Fire Code Lawsuit Brought Dismaying Side Effects," *Washington Post*, February 18, 1997, sec. A, p. 9.

2. See Karyn Spellman, "Becton Finds First Six Months Full of Surprises; Critics See Little School Progress," *Washington Times*, Friday, May 9, 1997, sec. C, p. 8. Valerie Strauss and Sari Horowitz, "Confusion Still Rules in D.C. Schools; Who Is in Charge Remains Question," *Washington Post*, May 31, 1997, p. B1.

3. U.S. Department of Education, National Center for Education Statistics, Laurie Lewis and others, *Condition of America's Public School Facilities 1999*, NCES 2000-032 (Department of Education, 2000), pp. iv–v.

4. Michael Sullivan, *Financing School Facilities* (Reston, Va.: Association of School Business Officials International, 1999).

5. Even when poor districts tax themselves at high rates, they struggle to find enough money to build and fix schools. *American School and University* (April 2000) (http://asumag.com/mag/university_class_struggle [June 2004]). Mike Kennedy explains how Isaac School District Number 5 in Phoenix, Arizona, could not afford to fix its schools despite having "the dubious honor of taxing its property owners at the highest rate" in the county.

6. Certificates of participation, like bonds, are tradable securities sold to investors to finance lease-purchase agreements. They are guaranteed by the lease between the district and the landlord and are repaid from the district's annual appropriations to the landlord. They are not a long-term obligation (and therefore not debt), a technicality that permits districts approaching their debt limit to gain access to funds.

7. The opportunity cost of an asset can be thought of as the sum of the explicit costs associated with it (what it costs to maintain and so on) and its implicit costs or the sacrificed alternatives that we associate with owning it.

8. Christy Watson, "Accountability at Center of School Plan," *Sunday Oklahoman*, March 4, 2001, p. 6A.

9. Linda Darling-Hammond, Jacqueline Ancess, Kemly MacGregor, and David Zuckerman, *Inching toward Systemic Change in New York City: How the Coalition Campus Schools Are Reinventing High School* (New York: National Center for Restructuring Education, Schools, and Teaching, 1998).

10. See chapter 1 in this volume.

11. David Weimer and Aiden Vining, *Policy Analysis: Concepts and Practices*, 3d ed. (Prentice Hall, 1999), p. 178.

12. Sullivan, *Financing School Facilities*; and Paul T. Hill, Christine Campbell, and James Harvey, *It Takes a City: Getting Serious about Urban School Reform* (Brookings).

13. The National Clearinghouse for Educational Facilities' Resource Lists contain extensive examples and ideas on novel approaches to school facilities, ranging from financing options to facilities planning to building and classroom design (Washington).

14. This discussion draws heavily on conversations with and materials provided by Brian Douglas Scott and Ryan Mottau. Both were involved in the founding of the Portland Public Schools Real Estate Trust.

15. For a complete account of Portland's experience, see Brian Douglas Scott, "Learning to Grow and Growing to Learn: Connecting Policies for School Fa-

cilities and Urban Growth," unpublished dissertation, 2003, Portland State University.

16. Hill, Campbell, and Harvey, *It Takes a City.*

17. Scott, "Learning to Grow and Growing to Learn," appendix B.

18. Most states set limits on how much money a district can borrow. The limit is usually around 10 percent of the assessed value of nonexempt property in the district. Money spent on lease payments is generally not considered debt.

19. Again, officials would have to weigh the trade-offs. These options might provide access to capital and space, but they can also bring higher costs. Depending on the circumstances, leasing may be more or less economical than borrowing. See Dan Smit and Rose Hesse-Wallace, eds., *Alternatives for Financing School Facility Construction in Eugene Public School District 4J,* (Eugene, SD 4J Research, Analysis, and Planning, 1980). For more detail, see Governor's Office of Planning and Research, State of California, *A Planner's Guide to Financing Public Improvements* (www.ceres.ca.gov/planning/financing/chap6.html#chap6 [August 2000]).

20. See Jeffery Lackney, *Thirty-Three Education Design Principles for Schools & Community Learning Centers* (Starkville, Miss.: Educational Design Institute, Mississippi State University).

21. Donald Kettl, "Managing Indirect Government," in *The Tools of Government: A Guide to the New Governance,* edited by Lester Salamon (Oxford, 2002), p. 491.

22. Ibid., p. 500.

23. Ibid., p. 508.

FIVE   *Incubators for*
New Schools

ABIGAIL WINGER

WHETHER LAUNCHED BY school districts, entre-
preneurs, religious groups, or charter school advocates, starting a school
is no easy task. It is certainly not something that can be done with
little thought or planning. Yet traditional approaches to new school
start-ups have entailed little more than providing a building, inserting
staff, and replicating existing programs and policies. The results, especially in big-city school districts, have been predictable, as the schools
do no better than the ones they were meant to replace. The ensuing
failures of many such schools raise questions about the merits of this
start-up model.

Private and charter schools are not immune from problems, either.
When nontraditional founders sponsor new schools with unique, localized programs, many of them face challenges working through the unfa-
miliar process of school start-up. Especially in the growing arena of
charter schools, teachers, parents, administrators, and board members
often need some time to reach agreement on what they want from the
school. When that agreement has been reached, it is not unusual to see
some parents separate from the school.[1]

Difficulties with school start-up and the desire to create effective schools
have stimulated the creation of school incubators in a few localities such
as Milwaukee, Wisconsin, and Dayton, Ohio. A school incubator invests
in the development of new schools before they open. It gives groups of
school administrators and teachers a time and place to work together to
receive expert help and advice long before they have to open new school

41

doors. In an incubator, groups slated to open a new school or take over an existing one can
—Find and adapt facilities to fit the instructional program;
—Learn how to manage their financial and legal responsibilities;
—Explore how they will select and prepare teachers;
—Try out and choose instructional materials and approaches;
—Choose sources of ongoing advice and assistance;
—Develop materials to explain the school to parents and students; and
—Decide how they will assess and demonstrate performance.

Outsiders might wonder how these functions are carried out without an incubator. The answer is that, unfortunately, too often they are not done well, if at all. School start-up can often be rushed, with more time spent on the operational, rather than the educational, aspects of the planning process. Teaching staffs are sometimes assembled just days before students arrive. New school personnel are then often forced to run the school through trial and error, on the job, which is clearly to the detriment of their students.

Public school systems seldom take responsibility for creating incubators, and, since pressures for current services and teachers' pay always outweigh the forces in favor of investing in them, it is unlikely that they ever will. Creating such institutions in big cities could be enabled by philanthropy. Philanthropies can also provide seed money so that teachers, principals, and parents hoping to start new schools can pay the fees charged by incubators and buy other materials and equipment required to support their planning.

New school incubators are based on the successful model of the business incubator. In the private sector, incubators are generally designed to reduce the risk of start-up by providing access to resources and expertise otherwise unavailable to entrepreneurs. While schools maintain significant differences from businesses, the many similarities in both organizations' start-up challenges and support needs lead to the recognition that developers of a school incubator can learn from the structure of existing business incubators.

Based on interviews I conducted in 2001 with eight founders of new schools (public and private) and five directors of business incubators, and a review of the literature, it seems clear that the case for new school incubators is compelling.[2]

The Growing Need for New Schools

Many circumstances indicate the need for new, and often different, schools, including the following:

Enrollment growth. The primary driving force behind the need for new schools is growing student population. In high schools alone, there is an estimated need for an additional 1.3 million places in the coming decade.[3] Current building capacity is not adequate. In the next decade, for example, the state of Washington's K–12 population will increase by 200,000 students, creating the need for an estimated 340 new schools.[4]

Policies to turn around failing schools. The accountability and standards-based reform movement has also created a need for new schools. By 1999, seven states had passed legislation allowing them to take over academically bankrupt schools.[5] This trend is likely to accelerate under the accountability provisions of the federal No Child Left Behind legislation. Many schools have been reconstituted by their districts, which also have the authority to reconstitute or redesign failing schools.[6] Done well, reconstitution can mean a positive start for a redesigned school with a good chance for a successful turnaround. Done poorly with little preparation or assistance, it is almost surely a waste of time and money. An incubator can improve the chance of successful school turnarounds.

Growth of the charter school movement. More evidence of the need for new schools has arisen from the growth of the charter school movement. By 2004, there were 2,996 new charter schools in the forty-one states (including the District of Columbia) that had enacted charter school laws.[7]

Increased preference for smaller schools. The rising popularity of small schools and of schools-within-schools is another indication that many more new schools may be needed in the future. Based on research linking small school size to improved student achievement, safer school environments, better-served special-needs students, and encouragement of teachers' innovation and ownership, the Department of Education and foundations such as the Bill and Melinda Gates Foundation have chosen to promote small schools in recent years. By the end of 2003, the Gates Foundation had awarded $373 million in grants to create new small high schools.

Challenges of School Start-Up

In spite of the growing demand for new schools, they are not easy to create. Lack of capital and start-up financing and insufficient operational expertise are some of the barriers that make it difficult to open and operate new schools. Although ample research exists about how schools fail once in operation, little information is available about the process of starting new schools. Aspiring founders face several common barriers, including little access to resources and technical expertise, lack of start-up financing, no time or space for planning, and inability to find others with experience in starting schools.

Resources and Technical Expertise

Most school founders were inexperienced with school start-up and operation and did not know to get the advice and tools they needed. They often had little technical expertise with marketing, financial planning, legal regulations, or how to gain access to available resources. Some founders (typically, parents and teachers) were not aware of the support that was available. At other times, schools were denied access to needed resources because districts were pressured by the community to start a new school, which they did with little enthusiasm. One public school administrator dealing with the frustrations of creating a new public school said: "I needed complete and full district support and communication, and assistance, and someone at the other end of the phone willing to pick it up and provide an answer and get someone out here to help you. . . . I think many school district administrations around the country are not actually managerially equipped to do this sort of thing. I mean that kindly. I think they're not equipped to do this. I think this is too hard, too challenging, and too unknown."

Start-Up Financing

Another barrier to launching a school is revealed in the lack of start-up financing available for planning, programs, or building renovation or construction. One parent dedicated fourteen years to the creation of a new Catholic high school. The process took that long because of difficulties obtaining space. After he went through the arduous process of securing financing to build a new facility, he could not find a suitable interim school. Inevitably, the school experienced numerous delays once it was under construction. Many other founders noted the difficulty of finding funding for the school building, and several wound up temporarily housed in trailers. One public school principal said: "Districts are reluctant to give you the start-up funds that you need to put you on an equal footing with an up and running school. That means all of a sudden front-loading 80 computers. That means popping a library in. That means giving you all your textbooks at once for all your kids. . . . I have no resource center. I have no supplies. I could take you into my room and at least 10 of my student desks are so wobbly you'd be afraid to sit in them. All of my desks come from some warehouse somewhere. We don't have new equipment. . . . No teacher on this staff had a working computer for the first year of this school."

Time and Space for Planning

New school planners also have a difficult time finding time and space for the planning process. Since an education program, brand-new policies and procedures, and a financial plan often have to be created, planners mentioned that this process required more than the several half-days of shared release time. Yet, in many districts, that is all the paid time teachers have to work together. One public school founder felt that she would have liked longer blocks of planning time instead of sporadic monthly meetings. She also noted that the planning group needed a location where they could gather and devote time to planning together instead of just using e-mail.

Time constraints are just as much of an issue for private school founders. One parent, concerned with the quality of her local public middle school, pursued the creation of a private all-girls middle school, cofounded with other parents. She lamented that her school will not be able to expand because the parent founders just do not have the time to put into the process.

Accessing Others with Start-Up Experience

New school founders had little or no connection to others who had started, or were in the process of starting, a school. They also lacked links with districts needing schools, making it difficult to find a sponsor for the school. The lack of access to other founders was a missed opportunity for all, resulting in time wasted, best practices uncaptured, and networking and mentoring opportunities lost.

From this lack of connection grows a more fundamental issue: models of a planning process are not readily available. Parents and teachers with good intentions and ideas often have no idea what the planning process for school start-up should consist of or look like. They do not know how to anticipate the problems in the planning process or with the initial school start-up phase. This can lead to delays, avoidance of difficult issues, greater than average chaos the first year of the school, and sometimes closure.

The Concept of Incubation

Given the increasing need for new schools and the risks and difficulties in the school start-up process, new school incubators are important tools to help overcome the barriers to school start-up. A new school incubator is an adaptation of the business incubator—an organization formed to accelerate the development of potentially successful entrepreneurial companies by providing hands-on assistance and various business and technical support services during the vulnerable early years. For more than two decades, business incubators have contributed to entrepreneurial activity in the United States by creating conditions favorable to the development of new firms. Early incubators focused on the service and manufacturing sectors, while incubators focused on technology-based companies have grown in importance within the past decade.[8]

Business experts define "incubate" to mean maintaining "under prescribed and controlled conditions an environment favorable for hatching or developing. It also means to cause to develop or to give form and substance to something."[9] Therefore, to incubate a fledgling company or school implies prescribing and controlling conditions favorable to the development of a successful new organization.

Typically a business incubator provides space for a number of businesses under one roof while the groups create business plans, find customers, and launch their products. Business incubators reduce the risk involved in business start-ups because their young tenant companies gain access to facilities, equipment, and expertise that might otherwise be unavailable or unaffordable.[10] A school incubator holds the same promise of reducing risk to new schools by providing access to resources and expertise. The success of business incubators provides a rationale and a model for the creation of a new school incubator.

Start-up companies need incubation owing to the high risk of failure of entrepreneurial start-ups. Nearly 50 percent of small businesses are thought to fail within five years, although small business experts warn that this figure is likely inflated by the filing of papers to establish firms, proprietorships, and corporations that are never actually established. Such "small businesses" do not fail; they are never launched.

Business incubators vary in the scope of assistance provided to entrepreneurs.[11] Incubators share some common components, however, such as flexibility in the leasing and management of space, centralized services to reduce overhead costs, and various types of business assistance. Incubators may offer low-cost office and laboratory space, administrative services, access to library and computer facilities, skilled consultants, an inexpensive workforce in the form of graduate and undergraduate students, and special contacts with bankers, venture capitalists, technologists, and government officials. This environment gives entrepreneurs the freedom to be creative with product development since financing and organizational management are supported by the incubator. An incubator may also provide secretarial support, copy services, accounting services, technical editing help, computer equipment, conference space, health and other benefit packages, and access to university facilities.

Whatever the services offered, the goal is always the same: to produce successful and sustainable "graduating" businesses. Although hardly an unbiased source of evidence, the National Business Incubation Association (NBIA) reports that business incubators are enjoying some success. One study sponsored in part by NBIA found that graduates of business incubation programs have higher than standard survival rates, with 87 percent of graduates still in business compared with the standard 50 percent survival rate, and most of these firms have been in business for at least five years.

Lessons Learned from Business Incubators

The success of the business incubator design points to lessons a new school incubator should heed since new schools and start-up businesses face many of the same challenges. Both can benefit from access to consultants, contacts, space, and networks with consumers (parents or districts, in the case of schools). Successful businesses and successful schools also share important characteristics (table 5-1). These similarities suggest that incubation, a method for dealing with businesses' start-up challenges, might also work for schools.

During interviews with directors of business incubators, the important guiding principles of running an effective incubator became clear. These principles can be translated into the following recommendations for school incubators.

Determine a clear mission and set realistic expectations. The mission is the core component of an incubator's program and structure. An incubator must be clear about its expectations and objectives in order to structure its program. The mission also needs to be updated over time.

Table 5-1. *Shared Characteristics of Successful New Organizations*

Successful entrepreneurs	Founding teams of successful new schools
Cooperative management team with a wide range of knowledge and skills	Diverse skills ranging from curriculum to budgeting to legal issues
Sound early financing	Financing to plan and to obtain and equip a school building
Focus on a lead product or service	Focus on a specific mission for the school—not a school that is "everything for everybody"
Decisionmaking informed by the market	Decisionmaking based on need and potential market rather than on "dream school"
Knowledgeable about best practice	Access to knowledge, experience, and best practice from diverse sources to use in the school plan
Business plan that provides direction and focus	Clear, thorough school design plan that uses the school's mission to inform the rest of its structure
Good money managers	Sound understanding of the available budget and ability to create a vibrant program within these constraints
Effective, entrepreneurial communicators, passionate about product or service	Enthusiastic, effective communicators of the mission and goals of the school to stakeholders (parents, teachers, students, school board, funders, and news staff)

Decide whom the incubator should serve. Deciding which clients to serve should flow directly from the incubator's clear mission. To fulfill its mission, an incubator must target specific clients. In choosing clients, incubators need high standards for entry, based at least as much on the soundness of the client's organizational plan and its demonstration of potential viability as on the specifics of the client's product.

Evaluate success. An incubator with an established mission and criteria for whom to serve should have a means of evaluating success, which must be clearly defined by the tenant and the incubator. It is important for an incubator and tenant to discuss the expected goal of the incubation so that there is no later confusion in determining a business's readiness to leave. Clarity is important because individuals housed in incubators often have varied definitions of success. If the incubator and tenant do not define standards for success, they will be unable to evaluate their performance.

Establish funding sources that fit the incubator's mission. Business incubators are financed through a combination of government funding, space rental fees, and fees-for-service. Foundation funding plays a small part in some incubators' incomes. Many incubators charge below-market-rate rent in an attempt to bolster small businesses. But others disagree with that philosophy, believing that rent is the smallest component of many business expenses and that something is wrong with a start-up that cannot absorb the costs of renting space.

Provide limited but useful services. Incubators should not try to do everything. According to the interviews, an incubator should emphasize four main functions: encouraging collaboration and networking, limiting services to a finite incubation period, helping locate sites for clients, and providing access to capital financing.

Ten Recommendations for a School Incubator

Ten key lessons, based on the experience of business incubators, might be applied to those who want to create school incubators:

—Set a clear mission for the incubator along with realistic expectations about what constitutes success.

—Clarify whether the incubator will help new school founders with planning or with start-up or operations as well. Help with planning seems to be a *de minimis* function of any incubator. But beyond that, will the incubator assist with operations in the first year or two? The pressure to do so will be enormous, and incubator developers need to think carefully about how, and under what circumstances, they are willing to help the school hatched in the incubator once it spreads its wings.

—Align entry requirements with the incubator's mission. Create clear and rigorous standards for which potential school start-ups the incubator will provide services.

—Rely on demonstrated demand for new schools (and new kinds of schools) before launching an incubator.

—Assert a viability mentality. Incubators should support not only schools that fit its mission but also schools that have the leadership required to develop good financial plans and budgets. Incubating "nice ideas" is not enough; an effective incubator should be helping develop schools that are still educating children ten years after they leave the incubator.

—Focus on people not programs. Educational incubators, like their business counterparts, should focus on finding people with the skills to create and run a coherent program. As such, they should be paying a lot of attention to the educational philosophy of potential leaders.

—Evaluate success. Think about indicators for graduation and how the incubator will know a planning team is ready to leave the nest. Track graduates of the incubator. Did they implement the plans they hatched in the incubator? Are they still offering services five or ten years down the line? Or have they disappeared? What impact have they had on student achievement?

—Consider how to finance the incubator. Will fees from planning teams be a source of income? Will the incubator offer space to hold classes or launch a school? If so, what will it charge? What sources of financial support for the incubator are available from state and local educational agencies? From foundations? And from fees for service? It is just as important to think about how the incubator will finance itself as it is to consider how the clients will finance their programs.

—Try to link supply and demand. Conceivably, an incubator with well-tuned antenna could help match new school ideas with districts and communities interested in them. The incubator could also help connect new school creators with those who have already successfully opened a school.

—Help new schools obtain financing. Many new school directors are inexperienced in the intricacies of school finance. Obtaining financing is always an integral part of the school start-up process and, at a minimum, a school incubator should serve as a clearinghouse to facilitate access to capital and operating funds.

Much of the nation's school reform effort relies on the supply of strong school organizations. Many schools, especially in big cities, have performed at such a low level for so long—and are so internally divided—that the only way to preserve children's learning opportunities may be to create promising new schools. Launching a new school is never easy. The process should not be invented anew every time a school is opened. If urban districts, state and local education agencies, and the philanthropic community can find a way to finance a network of new school incubators, the process promises to be a lot easier in the future than it has been in the past.

Notes

1. Paul T. Hill and Robin Lake, *Charter Schools and Accountability in Public Education* (Seattle: Center on Reinventing Public Education, 2002).
2. Quotations in this chapter are based on those interviews.

3. Richard W. Riley, "Annual Back-to-School Address: Changing the American High School to Fit Modern Times" (Washington: National Press Club, 1999), p. 1.

4. Robin Lake and Paul Hill, *Proposal to the Stuart Foundation* (Seattle: Center on Reinventing Public Education, 1999), p. 2.

5. "Quality Counts '99: Rewarding Results, Punishing Failure," *Education Week*, vol. 18, January 11, 1999.

6. Ibid.

7. "Number of Operating Charter Schools Up Ten Percent" (Washington: Center for Education Reform, February 11, 2004).

8. Louis Tornatzky, Hugh Sherman, and Dinah Adkins, "A National Benchmarking Analysis of Technology Business Incubator Performance and Practices" (Department of Commerce, 2002), p. 4.

9. Richard W. Smilor and Michael D. Gill, *The New Business Incubator: Linking Talent, Technology, Capital, and Know-How* (Lexington Books, 1986), p. 1.

10. *Business Incubator Project Overview* (Seattle: Urban Enterprise Center, 1998), p. 5.

11. For an international perspective on the value of business incubators, see Albert Philippe, Michel Bernasconie, and Lynda Gaynor, *Incubation in Evolution: Strategies and Lessons Learned in Four Countries* (Washington: National Business Incubation Association, 2004). Translated from the French, the study is a descriptive look at how business incubation works in France, Germany, England, and the United States.

SIX   *Taking Advantage of*
           Teacher Turnover

SARAH BROOKS

PAUL T. HILL

A NATIONAL TEACHER shortage is always just around the corner, but it is not here yet.[1] Demand does outstrip the supply of teachers with good training in mathematics, science, and special education, but no overall shortage exists. No Child Left Behind legislation, however, may finally bring home the long-predicted teacher shortage, according to recent news accounts.[2] The new law requires that as a prerequisite to receiving federal assistance under Title I, all new teachers in the school district be licensed and certified in their fields.

Some districts have trouble finding enough teachers of all sorts, but these are usually inner-city districts right next door to suburban districts that have many applicants for every vacancy. Urban schools and districts do not compete very successfully for talented and well-educated young people. Big cities often make job offers much later in the year than do nearby suburban districts, largely because of elaborate "bumping" processes that guarantee senior teachers the right to claim open jobs before anyone new is hired.[3] Some district Human Resource departments screen out the best-educated applicants, preferring to hire teachers from less demanding colleges and academic majors who are more likely to "fit in."[4] Candidates have to navigate a bureaucratic hiring maze, and new teachers often find themselves thrown into the most difficult teaching situations. These facts can make teaching unattractive for the ablest college graduates, who also have other, often higher-paying, job opportunities and who prefer to be paid for displaying imagination and creativity, not attributes rewarded by teaching's seniority-based pay scale.

52

Add to these realities a labor market in which new graduates now anticipate having several careers and moving among occupations and employers in search of opportunity and income, and teaching in big-city school districts looks uncompetitive. As the *New York Times* recently reported, teaching attracts a shrinking proportion of the ablest college graduates.[5] Though on average teachers are now about as able as ever before, the distribution of ability is truncated, with less able people excluded by stricter licensing rules and the more able drawn off into other pursuits.

The teaching profession in general, and urban districts in particular, needs to attract greater numbers of good people. That means teaching must become more attractive to the able people whose career expectations do not include lifetime employment in a rigid civil service structure. Finding a solution will not be easy. Small changes in teachers' pay and aggressive recruiting campaigns might have some effect, but real solutions must address the basic liabilities of urban districts as employers.

This chapter and the next suggest ways of improving the flow of able people into teaching and the principalship, arguing for fundamental changes in recruitment, training, and career development far beyond the capacity of existing district hiring and human resource development institutions. These changes require wresting hiring and career development from district insiders who have strong incentives to reproduce themselves and avoid introduction of people who will challenge the status quo. They also recognize that urban districts must compete in a metropolitanwide labor market. This fact has positive implications—districts can look beyond their own boundaries to find promising people—and negative ones—city districts must compete for the best people with others that have more money, simpler politics, and fewer challenging schools.

Redefining the Potential Labor Force

One perennial proposal for improving the intake to teaching is the "two-pathways" strategy. The first pathway is the one we have now, for individuals committed to a lifelong teaching career. The second is for individuals interested in serving as teachers for a limited time and then moving into other careers—and possibly back to teaching at some point. Arthur Wise described such a "two-tiered" model in his 1986 article, "Three Scenarios for the Future of Teaching."

The proposal would structure the teaching profession like the U.S. Army during the time of the draft when "a permanent and fairly well-paid cadre of professional officers and noncommissioned officers inducted, trained, and supervised ever-changing contingents of drafted or enlisted recruits, who remained in the Army for relatively short periods."[6] Similar professional and enlisted positions could be developed in teaching. Wise argued that an approach emphasizing differentiated roles had some benefits: it might allow for potentially significant pay increases for career teachers, and its loosening of some of the requirements to become a "temporary" teacher might ensure more interested and talented candidates during shortages.

Others described similar models. The prestigious Holmes Group, for example, called for a dramatic differentiation of teachers' roles, including positions like "career professionals," "professional teachers," and a new tier of "instructors" who served in a temporary, highly supervised entry capacity.[7] In the early 1990s, Harvard University's Richard Murnane questioned the practicality of a system based on career-long retention of all teachers, arguing that it could deter some highly qualified potential teachers from entering the field because of their uncertainty about making a long-term commitment to the profession.[8]

Models like the two-tiered model and the Holmes Group's blueprint offered only limited roles for shorter-term teachers. These "temporary" teachers would be allowed only to implement prescribed curriculums overseen by career teachers. Shorter-term teachers were, in the end, second-best alternatives—not assets for enhancing students' experience in the classroom. Turnover was, in short, an unfortunate part of the labor market for teachers—a liability to be controlled and constrained.

This need not be the case. In-flowing teachers can be more than implementers of "teacher proof" curriculums, especially if they are selected with care, supported, and given appropriate but meaningful responsibility. Many private, charter, and parochial schools have survived with mixtures of whole- and partial-career teachers. They induct new entrants, leverage what all of their teachers bring to the classroom, and support shorter-term and career teachers in ways that create effective learning environments for their students.[9]

We think it is possible to envision a human resources strategy that considers an inflow and outflow of highly skilled and talented individuals as something positive that helps create new and varied learning opportunities for students.[10] Current conditions in the general labor market, the teaching profession, and public education reform signal that incorporating turnover as an asset may be an idea whose time has come.

General Labor Market Condition

A strong general economic boom and tight labor market, where college graduates had their pick of job opportunities, characterized the late 1990s, highlighting a trend that had been developing for a generation. Even in the more economically straitened 2000s, switching from job to job is often a feature of modern work life, for professionals and nonprofessionals alike.[11]

The average worker today has at least nine jobs between the ages of eighteen and thirty-four, with at least three jobs between the ages of twenty-five and twenty-nine and 2.4 jobs between ages thirty and thirty-four.[12] In some sectors, turnover has become the norm. As a result of dramatic shifts in the labor market, younger people beginning their careers expect more job mobility than earlier generations. Even midcareer professionals are choosing not to stay with one employer for the duration of their careers.

As job changing becomes more commonplace and acceptable (and at times, even a recognized route to professional growth), the lure of a career-long commitment to any occupation—including teaching—does not have the almost universal appeal it once had. Potential teachers—recent college graduates or midcareer professionals—may be much more comfortable with transitions from one career to another. An educational human resource strategy that ignores emerging career flows may drive away people who might have become good teachers at least for a period in their careers.

Conditions in the Teaching Profession

Changes in today's labor market for teachers exhibit several characteristics that may make working with turnover more attractive. For example, interest in teaching among individuals who have worked in other fields and sectors is growing. As one reporter noted, "Career switchers are the fastest-growing group in teacher training today."[13] In turn, many schools and districts recognize that a mid- or late-career candidate's maturity, relevant professional experiences, and disciplinary knowledge (especially in high-need subject areas like math and science) make him or her a very desirable candidate.[14] Districts might prefer, all things equal, to recruit a traditional candidate with comparable career experience. But all things are not equal, and many districts settle for something a great deal less, that is, converted teachers' aides who lack college degrees, or completely inexperienced college graduates.

Compared with other professions and careers, teaching has lost some attractiveness. In a high-paced, high-demand economy, school salaries lag behind compensation in other occupations. The result is that although potential teachers may be interested in teaching for a number of years, many may find that the opportunity costs of doing so for decades are too high. High-ability candidates may be willing to forgo high salaries for a few years but not for their entire career.

Economic Change and School Reform

As our economy changes, demand for more "knowledge" workers grows, putting a premium not only on students who can perform basic skills but also on the ones who can solve problems and learn throughout life. Knowledge of the subject matter, an understanding of the developmental needs of students, an ability to make real-world connections, and the ability to harness the power of new technologies are key elements in teaching today. Bringing in new and midcareer candidates and supporting them with longer-term career professionals may provide the necessary mix of pedagogical understanding, knowledge of subject matter, and real-world applications to ensure that our teaching workforce can provide students with these learning opportunities.

The Potential Benefits of Managing Teacher Flow

Effective management of the flow of people into and out of teaching could offer some important benefits. Districts could expand their potential labor market, protecting themselves against cyclic declines in the numbers of teachers available from conventional education schools. A flow of teachers could broaden the perspectives and world experiences brought into the classroom. A teacher who has had to write business reports or figure out the ratios involved in assigning profits among partners, for example, could answer the query "Why do I need to learn this grammar (or algebra) anyway?" with tangible examples from work experience.

The teaching profession would reap some benefits too. One would be a special status for career "lead" teachers. Such status would require a differentiated career path that recognizes the different strengths and expertise offered by shorter-term and longer-term teachers. Since many schools' faculties would have a mix of teachers with different experiences, it will be possible to give significant pay increases to the smaller number of teachers who assume roles requiring the greatest experience and expertise. Career teachers would not have to move out of the classroom for pay increases and increased respect and responsibilities; instead, they could move into a position that recognizes and makes use of their expertise and experience.

Ironically, opening teaching to more potential candidates may increase respect for the profession. As more people with teaching experience make a transition into other jobs, employers and colleagues will have a chance to recognize the skills of those individuals who have been teachers. The formal evaluation systems that will be essential to maintaining a quality teaching workforce will necessitate the creation of professional standards or expectations for effectiveness. Such expectations and standards of professional achievement will be important in elevating the prestige of teaching.

Finally, a strategy to work with the flow of teachers can improve schools' and districts' relationships with their broader community. As more workers flow into and out of teaching, more community workplaces will have connections with those people who have been teachers. Moreover, schools can establish explicit relationships with some workplaces, providing exchange programs through which the scientist at the high-tech research firm can teach high school classes, and the high school science teacher can develop hands-on research experience. Such mutually beneficial relationships are possible when new options for entering teaching and new definitions of being a teacher are created.

Institutionalizing Management of Teacher Flow

Managing teacher flow is not the same thing as inviting anyone who is vaguely interested in teaching into the classroom. It would require concrete and deliberate changes, first in the ways that districts hire and assign teachers, and then in how they support, evaluate, and outplace them. Developing such a turnover strategy will require facing some difficult issues:

—Ensuring some basic entrance qualifications, while encouraging competent people with unconventional backgrounds to consider teaching;

—Providing essential training, without making the opportunity costs for entering teaching too high;

—Balancing the skills, knowledge, and expertise of career teachers with the experience and knowledge of "transitional" teachers; and

—Managing outflows, making sure that ineffective teachers leave early and that effective teachers who want to pursue other careers have options for leaving teaching.

A strategy that works with turnover should address these concerns with the following essential ground rules:

Develop alternative, strong pathways into teaching. All adults assuming responsible positions with students need to receive training and some form of certification in classroom management, pedagogy, and the art and science of teaching. But training opportunities and certification levels should vary, depending on the qualifications and career aspirations of the candidate. The midcareer professional who has a thorough understanding of chemistry will need different training and support before becoming an effective high school teacher than the recent college graduate well versed in educational theory and pedagogy. Both need training and both should receive it, but a one-size-fits-all training pathway that makes the opportunity costs of entering teaching too high for experienced candidates should be avoided.

Make the hiring process a locus for quality assurance. Working with turnover implies that more people will be recruited into teaching—as more people turn over, more people must be brought in. Some policy analysts have called for simply opening the floodgates and removing all the certification requirements and other "barriers to entry" to teaching to increase the supply.[15] One need not go to such an extreme to make sure the pool of potential candidates is large enough to ensure that schools can be very selective.

Some basic criteria for entry are essential—including college degrees, background checks, and willingness to participate in training. Above all, however, schools need to become discerning recruiters and selective hirers. The hiring process must accept much of the burden for quality assurance.

Currently, schools of education assume the primary responsibility for quality assurance. By overseeing certification, they, in effect, regulate access to licensure and thus entry into teaching. If different pathways are created, the burden of quality assurance shifts toward the point of hiring. To handle this burden responsibly, schools will need to experiment with hiring processes that meet their needs—this may include practice teaching sessions, more interviews with potential colleagues, and other opportunities to assess how an individual will handle teaching in real schools. Hiring decisions need more weight on the perceived ability of the individual to handle the job and less stress on uniform certification requirements.

Schools will need to build their capacity as smart and aggressive recruiters for talented teachers. Many schools and urban districts have begun to take more aggressive measures to recruit teachers, including nationwide and even international searches. Massachusetts has offered large signing bonuses to teachers from across the country.[16] When high-tech stocks were flying high, one gubernatorial candidate in Virginia promoted a scheme to attract teachers by offering them stock options from a pool established by the state's high-tech industries. More localities will need to learn how to make such efforts to ensure a pool of high-quality candidates from which to choose.

Differentiate and redefine the roles of teachers. Teachers who flow into and out of teaching will not be effective if they are confined to today's teaching roles. Schools will need new arrangements that take advantage of the different talents a mix of career and "transitional" teachers can bring to the classroom.[17]

Schools that employ shorter-term teachers and career teachers will want to consider having teachers work more collaboratively—the traditional one-teacher-one-classroom is not likely to lead to sound educational opportunities in these circumstances. Shorter-term teachers will need to be paired with career professionals so that both can learn from each other. The career professional can ensure that experience and expertise in teaching are transferred and present in the classroom, while the shorter-term teacher will bring in new skills and experiences that can add to the perspective and learning experiences for students. The key to this strategy will be identifying the comparative advantages of the different groups of teachers and creating teaching and school structures that support them working together.

All new teachers—whether on the career track or shorter-term track—need new opportunities and better support. They need intense induction and ongoing mentoring, so that they have a chance to truly learn what teaching is like and so that they can decide if they seek a shorter-term or longer-term career in teaching. Schools will then have a chance to thoroughly assess whether the current candidate is right for teaching. Such induction would be a dramatic shift from what typically happens today. In most schools now, a new teacher is immediately expected to do the same basic job—teach a class full of students—as a twenty-five-year veteran. In fact, new teachers are often given even harder assignments, in some of the most difficult schools, with students with the greatest needs. A strategy that tries to make some turnover an asset will have to avoid the "sink or swim" induction method of today.

Policy discussions about improving the profession frequently focus on teacher collaboration and purposeful induction as hallmarks of good practice. They are often, however. treated superficially in real schools. A human resource strategy devoted to ensuring that all teachers meet the needs of their students can push these important features beyond exhortation.

Evaluate performance not persistence. To ensure quality teaching, a strategy that relies on turnover will need to be vigilant about managing effective outflows.[18] Paths out of teaching need to be opened for ineffective teachers who are not meeting students' needs and for effective teachers who choose other career options after teaching.

Teachers receiving poor evaluations need to be "counseled out" of the profession. Thorough and fair teacher-evaluation mechanisms will be essential to ensure the integrity and effectiveness of the profession. Counseling out teachers who do not meet these expectations should be less risky for schools, since inflows to the system will have opened and qualified replacements can be anticipated.

Managing outflows, however, cannot be confined to moving out of the classroom only those who were not effective teachers. It should also assist those teachers who have served effectively and are now interested in another career. For example, school systems will need to provide teachers with greater freedom for mobility. Efforts to make retirement funds and other benefits portable, for example, will be important human resource strategies for school districts to consider. Coalitions of teachers unions and other professional employees associations could certainly provide valuable assistance in managing these important benefits.

Many of these proposed ground rules would be important in recruiting new teachers. Ironically, some of these ground rules, if implemented effectively, might reduce turnover (for example, offering induction opportunities that are truly supportive might inspire more teachers to stay through their first year, and differentiated career pathways might help teachers see options for meaningful promotion without leaving the classroom). In any case, a strategy based on working with turnover would need to take these essential first steps to ensure sound learning opportunities for students

Institutionalizing the Flow Model

Little if anything about the flow model just described violates state law. Alternative routes into teaching and provisions for midcareer entry and reentry into teaching already exist. Most districts can reward lead teachers for their special mentoring duties. The institutional challenges are within districts, either in the ways their central human resource units operate or in the provisions made to guarantee the placement rights of senior teachers.

District human resource offices are unlikely to change themselves, but superintendents and school boards can transform their missions, incentives, and structures.[19] In many districts, given the strength of old habits and entrenched individuals, a new human resource unit might be required. Such a unit need not be outside the existing central office line structure, but it might operate best in a new place, either as a staff unit reporting directly to the superintendent or as an independent organization operating under a performance contract.

Compared with existing district human resources offices, a staff unit reporting to the superintendent is more likely to support the district's overall school improvement strategy and to pay close attention to the needs of principals. If unit employees have term contracts or serve at the superintendent's pleasure, they are unlikely to join central office line units in resisting the introduction of needed outsiders.

Creating a new human resource capacity within a district might be extremely difficult, especially because it could be hard to avoid transferring many employees from the former office to the new one. It also would not take more than one inattentive superintendent for the new office to become captured by permanent employees or teachers unions. Thus, as in the other subject areas covered by this book, an externally managed capability would have greater independence and staying power.

A contracted-out human resource function can have these advantages and others. If one such organization served many districts, it could develop a broader pool of potential teachers than any single district could generate. It could readily inform district leaders about trends in placement of teachers—whether, for example, promising individuals tend to avoid one district or set of schools—and suggest ways of becoming more competitive.

Help and investment from business and philanthropy are also important. Large professional businesses—hospitals, law firms, software developers—live in a competitive labor market for highly educated talent, and their practices can inform school districts' human resource management. A new human resource management institution could take on problems that existing bureaucracies have excluded from consideration. A new institution can ask and seek answers to questions such as the following:

—What kind of training is necessary and efficient for midcareer entrants and college graduates who do not anticipate a life-long career in teaching? Can they be trained to provide meaningful learning opportunities to students? Who should provide such training?

—Is it possible to ensure that the benefits of welcoming a variety of highly qualified individuals into teaching will exceed the costs—to the candidates and the system—of investing in their training for three to five years of service?

—Are enough individuals interested in short-term teaching to make the inflows sufficient?

—How can the career teacher and the teacher offering service for a shorter period complement one another most effectively? How can the system ensure adequate mentoring?

—Beyond teacher certification, what other signals of potential teacher effectiveness can aid in the hiring process? What are the attributes of individuals who successfully teach after a career in another sector?

—Does the inflow of nontraditional teachers make sense at all grade levels? Are there distinctions between elementary and secondary education with implications for strategy?

—Under what circumstances might it make sense to consider such a strategy? What community assets are necessary? What are the barriers to effective outflows that must be considered?

—How are districts with shortages of prospective teachers dealing with the challenge of finding qualified candidates? Are their coping strategies effective? Do these districts have better or worse alternatives than a flow-based strategy?

Conclusion

Turnover can be an opportunity. It need not signal educational distress. Organizationally supported, expected, and even planned turnover among shorter-term teachers, combined with a core of experienced teaching professionals, could help address shortages of teachers. Institutionalizing such a strategy could conceivably enrich and expand educational opportunities for students.

Notes

1. Ann Bradley and Jeff Archer, "Help Wanted: 2 Million Teachers," Special Series on the Nation's Supply of and Demand for Qualified Teachers (March–April 1999), various issues.

2. Stephanie Banchero and Noreen Ahmed-Ullah, "U.S. Act Tightens Certification Rules," *Chicago Tribune*, March 26, 2002, p. 1.

3. Elizabeth Useem and Elizabeth Farley, *Philadelphia's Teacher Hiring and School Assignment Practices: Comparisons with Other Districts.* (Philadelphia: Research for Action, April 2004.)

4. Dale Ballou, "Do Public Schools Hire the Best Applicants?" *Quarterly Journal of Economics*, vol. 111 (February 1996), pp. 97–113.

5. Virginia Postrel, "In Their Hiring of Teachers, Do the Nation's Public Schools Get What They Pay For?" *New York Times*, March 25, 2004, p. C2.

6. Arthur Wise, "Three Scenarios for the Future of Teaching," *Phi Delta Kappan*, vol. 67 (May 1986), pp. 649–52.

7. The Holmes Group included education deans from major universities and colleges across the country. See Holmes Group, *Tomorrow's Teacher: A Report of the Holmes Group* (East Lansing, Mich.: Holmes Group).

8. Richard J. Murnane and others, *Who Will Teach?: Policies That Matter* (Harvard University Press, 1991). For other perspectives on turnover, see Ballou, "Do Public Schools Hire the Best Applicants?"

9. Dale Ballou and Michael Podgursky, *Teacher Pay and Teacher Quality* (Kalamazoo, Mich.: W. E. Upjohn Institute for Employment Research, 1997); and Ballou, *Do Public Schools Hire the Best Applicants?*

10. This chapter makes specific reference to secondary education because the in- and outflow of teachers with applied experience in subject areas seem most naturally suited for high school subjects. This is not to say, however, that elementary schools might not also consider such a strategy. Rather, additional research is necessary to determine if different human resource strategies are required for different levels of learning.

11. Ronald G. Ehrenberg and Richard S. Smith, *Modern Labor Economics: Theory and Public Policy* (Reading, Mass.: Addison-Wesley, 1996).

12. Bureau of Labor Statistics, "Number of Jobs Held, Labor Market Activity, and Earning Growth over Two Decades: Results from a Longitudinal Survey Summary," April 25, 2000 (http://stats.bls.gov/newsrels.htm [July 6, 2000]).

13. Valerie Marchant, "Why Not Teach Next?" *Time*, May 29, 2000.

14. Since 1984, forty-one states have created a total of sixty-eight alternative certification programs. Emily C. Feistritzer, "The Evolution of Alternative Teacher Certification," *Educational Forum*, vol. 58 (Winter 1994). National programs like Teach for America and Troops to Teachers have also emerged to train candidates.

15. See, for example, Frederick M. Hess, *Tear Down This Wall: The Case for a Radical Overhaul of Teacher Certification* (Washington: Progressive Policy Institute, 2001).

16. Ann Bradley, "States' Uneven Teacher Supply Complicates Staffing of Schools," *Education Week*, March 10, 1999, p. 1.

17. Several previous work groups, like the National Commission on Teaching and America's Future and the Holmes Group, and several innovative school districts (for example, Rochester, N.Y.) have proposed strategies for restructuring the teaching career pathway to create a career ladder. Revisiting some of these proposals might be a useful place to start looking for the specifics of how to

create a career pathway for long- and short-term teachers. Some of these models indicate that the salaries for "master" or "mentor" teachers can be significantly higher than the salary caps in teaching today. See National Commission on Teaching and America's Future, *What Matters Most: Teaching for America's Future* (Columbia University Teachers College, 1996).

18. See Ballou and Podgursky, *Teacher Pay and Teacher Quality*.

19. For an extensive analysis of district human resource offices' operations and potential contribution to school reform, see Christine Campbell, Michael DeArmond, and Abigail Schumwinger, *From Bystander to Ally: Transforming the District Human Resources Department* (Seattle: Center on Reinventing Public Education, 2004).

SEVEN   *Institutions to Find,*
Prepare, and Support
School Leaders

PAUL T. HILL

SARAH R. BROOKS

MOST CITIES REPORT difficulty finding enough
good principals: Seattle, for example, openly maintains a policy of rotat-
ing twenty-five outstanding principals among its nearly one hundred
schools. A 1998 survey by national principals' associations reported that
50 percent of districts nationally reported a shortage of qualified candidates for at least one principal opening in the prior year.

These "shortage" reports contradict evidence about the numbers of
people holding principals' certificates. As a series of studies sponsored by
the Wallace foundations has recently shown, every locality has enough
people with the formal qualifications, and all but a few districts are getting about as many applications for principalship openings as they ever
did.[1] Except for a few Sun Belt cities with exploding school populations,
the only localities unable to attract many seekers for each principalship
opening are central city districts in metropolitan areas where suburban
districts have plenty of applicants.

If there is anything to the reports of shortage—and there is—it has to
do with a mismatch between the current demands of the job, the qualities
of people nominally trained to fill it, and some districts' inability to attract the ablest people. District leaders say that the principalship has
changed, and people with traditional training and career backgrounds are
not up to the challenges.[2] All that is necessary to become qualified for the
principalship is to teach for a few years and to complete an educational
administration course at a university. Districts wait passively for people
with the necessary certificates to appear, hoping some will prove capable.

65

Many people take the training only to conclude the job is really not for them. Consequently, many people certified to work as principals avoid the job, preferring to stay in the classroom rather than take on daunting new responsibilities.[3]

Even in the absence of a true shortage, clearly good principals are scarce, and few school districts have any way to create or tap into a large group of potentially effective leaders. Pay differentials between principal and other top teaching positions are generally not large enough to encourage potential leaders to accept the stress and hassle of the principalship. And state regulations often prohibit districts from seeking other than the traditionally certified candidates for possible leaders.

How can communities find or develop effective leaders for schools? We believe that school districts can neither rely on colleges and universities to produce fully formed school leaders, nor trust themselves to do everything necessary to recruit quality leaders or support their career development. We see a need for foundation-funded institutions at the local and state levels to assume a permanent responsibility for helping solve this problem.

Role Confusion Is the Core Problem

School leaders should be able to coordinate the actions of adults so that all act in concert on behalf of children's learning. That job is hard to do in urban public education, where teacher turnover is high, adults have little incentive to break comfortable habits, and links between adult actions and children's learning are not carefully tracked.

More than anything else, urban public schools need consistency of effort and direction. Unfortunately, resistance to such focused leadership, from the district and within schools, is built into the rules, regulations, and traditions that have come to define urban public school systems. Today, these attributes of public school systems are seen as given, and efforts to strengthen leadership focus on helping educators cope with them. Effective and well-known principals in urban schools turn out to be immensely forceful individuals who take risks, ignore rules that interfere with performance, and play the politics of the system so well that others are afraid to challenge them.

This situation poses grave challenges for leadership development. Should school districts recruit and train people who can cope with the system as it is and accept its constraints? Should people be trained for leadership roles in which the people who make a difference must disregard the rules, hector others into actions they are not obliged to take, and do their most important work in opposition to the system? Accepting leadership positions as they are now guarantees that the individuals who hope to accomplish the most will be the most disappointed.

Are there better ways to prepare leaders for K-12 education? The answer is yes, but the best ways are not the most obvious. Retraining people self-selected for administrative posts in the existing system is not promising. Helping people learn how to cope in a system that does not reward initiative and assumption of personal responsibility does little for school quality or children's learning.

In an economy where bright people can usually find satisfying work, it is hard to see how enough potential leaders can be attracted and trained unless the jobs are redefined to offer more opportunities for satisfaction and accomplishment. Teachers unions and administrators' professional associations urge more investment in preservice training and better pay packages for teachers and principals. These changes might help slightly, but pay increases alone are unlikely to create a sufficient supply of leaders in K–12 education. Many potential principals and teacher leaders prefer lower-paying jobs to positions of leadership. (This chapter focuses on the principal's job. But a similar analytic approach would apply to the role of district superintendent.)[4]

School Leadership

The school head position is a problem for almost all forms of K–12 education.[5] Independent private schools can usually find competent heads, but they must often go through national searches and offer significant benefits packages. Parochial schools often have trouble finding good leadership too and can no longer rely on members of a religious order to supply it. Charter schools often go through a turbulent start-up period featuring a power struggle between the school founders and the hired school head; most charter schools wind up changing heads and governing boards as they mature. Big-city public schools, however, may have the most severe problems of all.

Headship of a school is a challenging and vulnerable position. An individual needs to exercise good judgment in adapting an academic program to the needs of the students in the school, maintain the confidence of parents and teaching staff, and avoid mishaps and scandals. Like any other chief executive officer, the school head is often praised for successes to which the head contributed little and condemned (or even fired) for failures he or she did not cause.

Though private and independent school heads carry more responsibilities than public school principals, they are often happier in their jobs and last longer than public school principals. How can someone who must worry about fund raising, admissions, establishing tuition levels (and collecting it), grounds maintenance, and hiring and promotion of teachers feel less burdened and more successful than someone who needs to worry only about the day-to-day operation of the school? There are many reasons, but they all boil down to the fact that in private schools, the heads' authority matches their responsibilities. They can delegate some of their responsibilities to others, over whom they have hiring and firing power. The private school head's role, however demanding and overwhelming in some situations, is relatively well defined.

That is not true in public schools. The responsibilities of the public school principal are defined by laws, regulations, and collective bargaining agreements.[6] Exhaustive definition, however, does not necessarily produce clarity. Today, every principal must live with four competing role definitions. He or she must be:

—The representative of the school board and the state government within the school, ensuring compliance with policies, rules, and collective bargaining agreements.

—The buffer between the school and the broader community, including the central office and school board, deflecting external demands away from teachers who can then work as they see fit.

—The broker and coordinator of teacher collaboration, facilitating but not dominating teachers' efforts to marshal the school's capacities on behalf of children.[7]

—An expert in the school's history and its instructional methods, the "keeper of the flame" about the school's distinctive mission and approach to instruction—the real instructional leader of the school.

Though one could imagine a person playing all of these roles, they are often incompatible in practice. The first role puts the principal's time and energy entirely at the disposal of people outside of the school. The school board and central office can control the principal's time by demanding reports and presence at meetings. For many principals this demand can consume more than half of all available working time. The unpredictability of central office demands can also disrupt any schedule a principal might have made for meetings and work within the school.[8] Ironically, reforms intended to increase a school's freedom of action—for example, school-based budgeting—often lead to new central office pressures, as district central office staff demand meetings and written explanations about budget decisions that schools supposedly have the freedom to make.[9]

The second role—serving as the buffer between the school and broader community—is essential for any school head, but in an urban public school system it can define the principal as an outsider who has no real role in the leadership of the instructional program. This becomes a real problem, when with no consultation with the teaching staff and no expertise in the instructional methods used at the school, a person is assigned as principal. This role is also more likely to overwhelm public school principals than private school heads. Public schools are often much larger than private and independent schools, so the number of possible transactions with parents, suppliers, and neighbors aggrieved by student actions and all the rest is correspondingly larger.

More important, public school principals have fewer resources in dealing with issues raised by parents and community members. That principals are bound by many rules and contractual provisions and do not control funds or school priorities means that they can do less in response to demands.[10] That principals cannot count on central office "back-up" in conflicts over students' behavior also forces principals to negotiate at length with teachers, parents, and community members about issues that private school heads can resolve more quickly.

The third and fourth roles of the principal—serving as the coordinator of teacher collaboration and the "keeper of the flame" for the school's mission—are essential to leadership as we have defined it, that is, concerning the actions of adults on behalf of children's learning. Unfortunately, for the reasons just given, many principals do not get the opportunity, and some lack the ability, disposition, or training to play these roles.

There are serious mismatches between a principal's two "insider" roles and the ways principals are trained and selected. Most public school principals are trained intensively for the first two "outsider" roles—on the rules and regulations they must enforce, the ways collective bargaining limits their authority over teachers, and techniques of community relations. Few are trained to think of their school as a productive organization in which all human and other resources must be used flexibly toward one end: student learning.[11] Most are taught that the values of public education are not compatible with the kind of strict performance accountability created by parental choice and competition among schools.[12]

Most states' certification rules for principals favor people who will play the "outsider" roles. Becoming a de facto leader of one's school, or proving leadership ability in some other human service field, is not the way to become a principal.[13] School districts must choose among people who have gained state certification. In some localities, collective bargaining agreements also prevent schools from elevating a current staff member—even an assistant principal who holds the appropriate certificate—to the principalship. Such agreements guarantee that every job is open to every person who holds a principal's certificate, but they make it difficult for a school to sustain its momentum by promoting a successor from within.

Schools need heads who can lead staff in negotiating the whitewater of constantly changing social pressures and student needs. They do not need absentees or leaders who will defer to teachers' autonomy instead of insisting on instructional coherency. Providing the leadership needed by schools requires more than simple retraining of incumbent principals. It requires clarification of the principal's role and recruitment of people who truly want to lead instructional organizations, along with appropriately designed training.

Shortages of quality principals are caused by the system, not by the individuals who try, often valiantly, to work in it. Principals, to sum up, are expected to focus on the outside of their schools and the inside. They are expected simultaneously to implement legislation, put new policies into practice, administer labor contracts, and avoid scandals and charges of noncompliance—all while satisfying external constituencies. Meanwhile, on the inside, they are expected to make sure that no child is left behind, every student gets instruction according to current professional standards, and that different parts of the school combine to give students a coherent instructional experience.

It is too much for many people. To fulfill all these expectations, principals need more time and energy than is available to normal human beings.[14] Moreover, the outside responsibilities are often so compelling that principals feel forced to put aside their inside concerns rather than risk lawsuits, financial penalties, or legislative inquiries. The result is that the internal leadership tasks often do not get the attention they deserve. A related result is burnout—discouragement and sometimes bitterness, leading to indifference from individuals who once chose to work in education because they loved children and learning.

Why Is It Hard to Find Good School Leaders?

District conditions clearly affect the supply of principals. Even in Sun Belt areas where some urban districts cannot find the people they need, neighboring districts often experience no shortages. When districts cannot hire people, it is often because of a weak competitive position owing to poor working conditions, turbulent district leadership, or poor pay. Many inner city districts serve as minor league farm teams for suburbs with more money and less school turmoil.

The confused and overly demanding roles just described, which are more evident in big-city districts than anywhere else, create shortages. Omnicompetent people who could meet all the demands of the principalship can also do many other things, including running successful businesses, foundations, and nonprofits. People who drift into such jobs simply because they are the "next step up" on the education career ladder are often well prepared for the teaching or subordinate administrator jobs they leave but lack the skills and experience to succeed in jobs that require political and technical leadership.

Current state certification rules limit the supply of potential leaders, but they still admit many people who are not prepared to perform. The rules might also exclude from leadership positions many people who could make real contributions as principals. The experience of uncertified principals who lead charter schools (and of uncertified superintendents recruited from business and the military) is certainly not worse than that of certified people in similar positions. The conclusion is obvious. A strategy of leadership development needs to tap these sources of potential principals and superintendents.

District-Caused Shortages

As Marguerite Roza found, many districts have tried to increase the quality of new principals by hiring only the most mature and experienced applicants. However, the pool of people who have taught for fifteen or twenty years is small and inelastic, and older principals often retire after only a few years in the job.[15] "Piling on" the experience requirements ensures that desirable people will be harder and harder to find. Though many districts get up to 30 percent of their applicants from nontraditional sources, including professionals in other fields who lack certification as principals, they are extremely unlikely even to consider hiring these people. Add to this that human resource officers generally seek to hire people like themselves in experience, training, educational background, race, and gender, and "shortages" can increase even more drastically.

Mismatch between Training and Roles

Leaders are often not prepared for the jobs they must do. People who are taught "it's all about instruction" can be ill-prepared for the interest-balancing and conflict management that is the daily lot of principals and superintendents.[16] Successful leaders are taught to balance pressures and to distinguish goals (educational performance) from constraints (the need to handle political and legal demands). But many others are so unprepared for their outside responsibilities that they are forced to spend full time mastering them.

Lack of On-the-Job Support

Finally, the system expects leaders to emerge fully formed. It does little to keep the best people on the job, nurture promising careers, or help people bounce back and learn from survivable failures. A 1998 survey by the National Association of Elementary School Principals found that 60 percent of school districts say they are unable to pay enough to attract or keep qualified candidates.[17] Despite the widespread perception of shortages, only half of all urban districts have any principal recruitment or preparation program, and less than half (46 percent) have an organized mentoring or "induction" program for new principals. More often than not, new principals are assigned to their jobs and left to fend for themselves.

Like recruitment, induction and mentoring happen by chance. Newcomers are mentored if they are lucky enough to happen onto someone who will voluntarily coach them. Mentors are not rewarded financially, though many take private satisfaction from the performance of those they are mentoring. Newcomers who run into trouble are often reassigned, and some who have an unsuccessful experience as a principal are assigned to the district central office, never to return to the schools.

Are these patterns inevitable? Do all public and private sector organizations force leaders to cope with such confusing roles and rely as much on chance for the recruitment and career development of key leaders? Or are there alternative approaches to leadership that public schools might imitate?

How Other Organizations Get the Leaders They Must Have

For this chapter we sought to understand how organizations that live and die by the quality of upper- and mid-level leadership leaders approach leadership development. We looked at organizations that require a combination of two things: disciplined common effort toward universally understood goals; and initiative-taking and competent problem solving by the leaders of key suborganizations. We took advantage of earlier Rand studies of military organizations like the U.S. Navy, professional governmental organizations like the Department of State and its embassies abroad, and dispersed businesses with many self-contained operating units.[18]

None of those organizations is identical to a K–12 school system. But, like public education, they have defined system-level goals and priorities that require concerted effort by many organizations (ships, embassies, local plants, and schools) that must adapt intelligently to local circumstances. Like school systems, the success of these organizations depends on the competence, imagination, and dedication of the people closest to daily operations.

Four characteristics of leadership development in such organizations are striking. Perhaps the most important is clarity about role. Organizations that want leaders to be effective make sure they have the resources needed to do the job. They also make sure that leaders do not face conflicting incentives that might lead some to focus on tasks that have nothing to do with the organization's performance. Thus in business, for example, annual performance goals are set in a negotiation between small-unit managers and their superiors, in which goals and budgets are established. Upper-level managers want their subordinates to accept ambitious goals and low budgets, but bosses who want their subordinate units to succeed must make sure goals and resources are compatible. Similarly, upper-level managers understand that anything that distracts a small-unit manager from performance will in the end hurt the overall organization's financial bottom line or its reputation.

Upper-level managers make mistakes, and sometimes they expect more than can be delivered. But these mismatches must be relatively rare: organizations that cannot meet their goals are, by definition, failures. Nobody can succeed as a top manager by disabling subordinates or setting expectations that cannot be met. No top manager can succeed by constantly pulling subordinates away from productive tasks into work that wastes their time. The results sought *must* be clear, and some alignment between capacities and expectations must prevail.

The second characteristic, purposive recruiting, is also vital. When organizations depend on the leaders of small units, leadership development is not left to chance. Understanding that their organizations live and die on the performance of unit leaders, top managers pay close attention to recruitment and training. In the armed services, chiefs of staff manage elaborate systems for identifying and tracking the development of younger officers. In the Foreign Service, senior diplomats advance their own careers by building networks of mentees on whose loyalty and competence they can rely. Big businesses with far-flung organizations profile potential leaders and tap individuals who, in the organization's experience, have the greatest promise. They also reward current leaders for finding and bringing in promising newcomers.

Third, leadership-dependent organizations prepare people through developmental placements. They do not expect people to emerge from formal training ready to lead. Developmental placements are the norm. Many provide elaborate formal training (for example, in the military academies) and supplement the results of training through carefully designed sequences of placement throughout the organization. Young military officers rotate through operational, analytical, procurement, and training roles, and the most promising are assigned to shadow senior commanders.

The diplomatic service hires the most outstanding college graduates and then trains them almost entirely on the job through sequences of placement in different roles, in Washington and in embassies throughout the world. Young corporate executives are also required to move among roles and localities, so they understand their company's entire business. These processes help potential leaders understand how key units function and how skills and disciplines come together to produce the corporate product.

Characteristic four, just-in time training, is equally important. Leadership-dependent organizations understand that the demands of any job are unpredictable, and a new leader may need targeted training and advice. Ambassadors and military commanders can request and get job-specific training. They have access to consulting organizations and other sources of expert advice and can pay for consultants when needed.

At lower levels, including quite small units, leaders are nurtured within the organization, through mentoring and peer support arrangements. In the military, the State Department, and very large businesses, younger persons often enter leadership positions in cohorts, and they are encouraged to maintain the same peer group throughout their careers. Up-and-coming leaders—even those who may someday be rivals for the top positions—are also put into contact with one another and with slightly more experienced individuals, to ensure that future corporate leaders know one another and also know many different individuals who have succeeded in the jobs to which they might later be assigned.

Big-City School Districts Do Not Use These Methods

These leadership-development patterns in other leadership-dependent organizations stand in marked contrast to efforts in big-city school districts. With few exceptions, state and local school systems:

—Do not manage leadership role definitions: these are defined haphazardly as different policies, rules, contract provisions, and the sentiments of school board majorities change. Districts lionize heroic principals who can work effectively in spite of these drawbacks.

—Are seldom organized to identify and encourage potential leaders. Most depend instead on "self-starters" who decide on their own to take graduate courses leading to certification as administrators. Teachers who emerge as natural leaders of their schools cannot become principals unless they first complete multiyear certification courses.

—Do not send potential leaders through a series of developmental placements, other than to require potential principals to spend some time as assistant principals.

—Rely heavily on formal university-based training for potential leaders but can do nothing to ensure that leaders have the opportunity to learn new skills as they take on progressively more challenging responsibilities.

—Encourage, but seldom promote or support, long-term mentoring and networking arrangements for school leaders.

Marguerite Roza's study of principalship shortages revealed that smaller, wealthier suburban districts identify young teachers with leadership skills, encourage them to take principal training, assign them to successively greater leadership responsibilities, and find mentors for them. A few big-city districts, for example, Cincinnati, have developed "principals academies" to attract able young teachers toward the principalship. Houston's Annenberg Challenge also pays for "Leadership Academy," a local recruitment and mentoring center for potential principals.[19] The Danforth

Foundation's Forum for the American School Superintendent created its own Principals Academy to introduce principals to theories of early childhood learning and then created a grants program to update principals in participating districts on leadership for learning.

For the most part potential principals must do without the advantages of clear role definition, purposive recruitment, developmental placements, and ongoing formal training and networking. Districts usually rely on whatever training the colleges and universities offer and choose principals from among the self-starters who apply for vacancies. University education departments have long provided leadership development programs as prerequisites for administrative certification. Graduates of these programs often feel unprepared for their jobs. Individuals might seek out learning opportunities, find mentors, or create informal support networks. But state and local school systems seldom take responsibility for these activities. Self-starting individuals can also take advantage of university-provided professional development opportunities like forums or other shorter-term programs for the ongoing development of existing school and school district leaders.

Some national institutions have recognized the need for better recruitment, training, and career support. Foundations, including the Danforth and the Wallace-Readers' Digest Funds, have supported initiatives on training and networking. A few national universities, public and private, have stepped forward to encourage greater collaboration between the arts and sciences and professional schools and schools of education (for example, UCLA and Stanford). And some nonprofit organizations (for example, associations representing elementary and secondary school principals) have offered networking opportunities.

But these more thoughtful and powerful efforts are few and far between. Programs are tiny and highly localized, and the number of principals who can take advantage of them is very small. Moreover, the individuals who lead the most challenging schools in big-city school districts are often people who have gone to college locally and have worked their whole careers in one school system, moving up from the classroom to the school office. These individuals are not likely to benefit from scarce opportunities that can be accessed only by those who are aggressive, aware of options nationwide, and well funded.

Until such time as programs like those mentioned above are hundreds of times larger, there will be no substitute for local capacity to recruit, develop, and nurture school leaders.

New Institutions

The problems of leadership development are not new, and they have severely affected the performance of big-city public schools for some time. Districts have been unable to solve these problems because they are hamstrung by inherited ways of thinking about leadership and by laws, contracts, regulations, and bureaucracies that make strategic initiatives difficult.

Districts can create the necessary capacities to find, develop, and support school leaders, but these initiatives would require new organizations, incentives, and investments that few districts could manage. Districts also inevitably face the temptation to retread existing central office units, a tactic likely to maintain the status quo.

Two other reasons also explain why new institutional capacities need to be built outside district central offices: First, the market for school leaders is a regional one, with neighboring districts regularly hiring each other's best people. Central city districts are unlikely to invest very much in principal development if the best products end up in the suburbs. Second, school districts might not be the dominant employers of school leaders in the future, as charter schools, multischool Education Management Organizations, and new schools developed in response to the choice provisions of No Child Left Behind become more numerous.

One or more independent institutions to recruit, train, mentor, and support leadership development would have important advantages, not the least of which is that they could perform a service for the entire metropolitan labor market of matching people with jobs and informing districts when their job offers are not competitive. These organizations could offer their services to school districts and independent schools, for a service or membership fee. Districts could get a wider range of services than they now get from their central offices and pay little or nothing more than they now pay for their human resource bureaucracies. A metropolitan area might have two or more such organizations, some independent and others based in universities, so districts could get the benefits of competition.

But for such organizations to form, whether inside school districts or independently, somebody must invest in institutional and program development. With philanthropic support, a new metropolitanwide development institution for school leaders could perform the following functions:

Training incumbent principals to perform new roles. As Portin and Schneider have shown, many principals must play roles for which they are not well prepared. However, most urban areas have growing numbers of charter and independent school principals who have been forced to learn the financial, personnel, and competitive strategy skills that public school principals now need.[20] A new institution could make such principals into resources for the training of district-employed principals.

Current and former charter school leaders could also take on leadership of district-run public schools. If former charter school leaders were assigned to the most troubled public schools—the ones for which the district is desperate enough to see improvement that it will give the principal unusual discretion—new approaches to the school leader's role could be brought into the district.

A charters-driven transformation of the school leader's role would be slow. But like the process of paying off a big mortgage, it would make small but detectable changes that could accumulate over time. Foundation-sponsored efforts to develop charter school leaders could accelerate the process, as would new state laws encouraging districts to charter larger numbers of schools. The pressures of standards-based reform, which apparently are driving some incumbent principals into retirement, could also increase districts' openness to principals who have experience running less-regulated, performance-driven schools.

Preservice training. School districts and colleges of education are now locked into an uncomfortable partnership. Because colleges provide the training required for principal certification, school districts must hire their graduates. Because school districts hire their graduates, colleges do not criticize school districts or even alert principals in training to the internal contradictions in the roles they must play. Some conventional schools of education are questioning their own training programs, as in the words of one education school professor interviewed for this study, "I am tired of telling people they should try to do things that I know cannot all be done." Moreover, academic researchers are finding that principals are highly critical of their training, saying that they learn neither how to cope with the most important challenges of the job nor, in many cases, even that these challenges exist.[21]

The most entrepreneurial colleges of education are trying to adapt their training programs. These are small in number, however, as are new programs to train principals jointly in business schools and schools of education. Stanford, Harvard, and Northwestern universities are creating new modes of preservice training, but state colleges and local schools of education show little interest in following their lead.

Proprietary colleges and nonprofits dedicated to leadership development are far more likely to provide new forms of preservice training. The training programs developed by several emerging proprietary and nonprofit providers such as the KIPP schools, Edison, and New Leaders for New Schools could be reproduced at the local level. This would require foundation investment in creation of new training institutions and some subsidies to attract the first cohorts of students. Leaders of charter and independent schools, and dissident education school professors disenchanted with their institutions' programs, could become the faculties.

Recruitment. Some school districts are taking new recruitment initiatives—New York, Chicago, Houston, and Los Angeles, for example, are seeking experienced managers for "alternative certification" programs. However, these are relatively small and limited to a few very large districts. Moreover, many of them, like the Houston Leadership Academy mentioned earlier, are funded not by school districts but by combinations of national foundations (for example, Annenberg) and local philanthropies. They are also designed and operated by nonprofits that have greater flexibility and freedom from regulation than do school districts.

With such institutions, charter schools become potential avenues for recruitment of new leaders. Noneducators who take leadership positions at charter schools readily recognize their own lack of preparation, and many seek training. Properly approached by district leaders, these alternative principals may be willing to consider positions in conventional public schools. The circulation of private and charter school teachers into conventional public schools is well documented. Charter schools, and combinations of alternative teacher recruitment programs and nonprofit school networks like KIPP, can conceivably become recruitment mechanisms for new public school principals.

New regional school leadership preparation programs could open up principal recruitment in these ways, offering subsidized training for nontraditional candidates who need combinations of training and hands-on experience.

Developmental placement. School districts can place less experienced people in subordinate administrative jobs (for example, assistant principalships). But as principals interviewed in our Wallace-sponsored studies consistently say, these positions have limited and compartmentalized responsibilities, and they often do not prepare an individual to manage the diverse burdens of the principalship. However, once an individual has become a principal, developmental placements are difficult to arrange; placement is often driven by seniority, union contract provisions, or efforts to maintain diversity across schools in a district and in schools.

A new regional leadership development institution could promote developmental placements in several ways—offering clearinghouses through which principals could learn about leadership opportunities in surrounding districts, supporting "hiring forums" where school district leaders could meet potential principals from other districts, and providing career counselors who would advise principals about their developmental needs and the availability of relevant opportunities.

In states where all public school employees are in the same retirement and benefits systems, interdistrict moves can be relatively simple. However, in states where district systems are separate, and in localities where placement opportunities are driven by seniority within a particular district, district-run or independent leadership development institutions will need to negotiate benefit packages, like those for teachers discussed in chapter 6, that protect the employability of individuals who move among districts for the purpose of development.

Mentoring and networking. Dedicated younger principals seek mentors, and dedicated older ones provide mentoring. However, few school districts provide funding for the mentorship function or reward principals who perform it. Seattle is an example of a district that wanted to promote mentoring but could do so only by pulling a senior principal out of his school and into the central office. This individual, inundated with requests for assistance, can no longer run a school.

Ambitious individuals also develop peer groups that support them and help solve emerging problems in their schools. However, districts do not provide time or money for these activities, so the people most in need often work in isolation. There is no substitute for the kind of distributed mentoring system that exists in business, military, and diplomatic organizations like the ones just reviewed. All senior leaders are expected to mentor, are assessed for mentorship quality, and gain career advantages from it.

A new regional leadership development institution can reward good mentors. Mentors and mentees could be paid foundation stipends for the time spent working together, either during off-duty hours or in one another's schools. Foundations could also sponsor development of peer cohorts, consisting of individuals who entered the principalship in a particular year, or cross-district groups of principals in similar schools.

In Sum

New leadership development institutions can do a great deal to improve the supply of capable school leaders. They can help incumbent principals adapt to new roles, they can recruit and develop principals more aggressively, and they can allow districts to recruit from a much wider pool of candidates than their central office human resource units now produce. By acting on these possibilities, district and foundation leaders can help ensure that when this question is revisited in a decade, analysts are not still endlessly debating why schools cannot find the leaders they need.

Notes

1. See Marguerite Roza, *A Matter of Definition: Is There Truly a Shortage of School Principals?* (Seattle: Center on Reinventing Public Education, 2003).

2. These themes, as noted in chapter 5, also pertain to shortages and recruitment of teachers. See, for example, Howard Fuller, James Harvey, Christine Campbell, Abigail Winger, and Mary Beth Celio, *An Impossible Job? The View from the Superintendent's Chair* (Seattle: Center on Reinventing Public Education, 2003).

3. Susan Gates, *Who Is Teaching Our Schools? An Overview of School Administrators and Their Careers* (Santa Monica: Rand, 2003).

4. On the constraints affecting public school leadership, see Public Agenda, *Stay Ahead of the Game: Superintendents and Principals Talk about School Leadership* (New York: Public Agenda Foundation, 2002). See also Jacqueline P. Danzberger, Michael W. Kirst, and Michael D. Usdan, *Governing Public Schools: New Times, New Requirements* (Washington: Institute for Educational Leadership, 1992); Paul T. Hill, Christine Campbell, and James Harvey, *It Takes a City: Getting Serious about Urban School Reform* (Brookings, 2000); and David Kearns and James Harvey, *A Legacy of Learning* (Brookings, 2000).

5. Particular state laws and collective bargaining agreements define the title "principal" differently. We therefore use the more generic "school head" in this chapter and reserve the use of the term "principal" to refer specifically to traditional public school heads.

6. On problems of urban public education governance and possible remedies, see National Commission on Education Governance Reform, *Governance for Better Schools* (Denver: Education Commission of the States, 1999). See also Paul T. Hill, Lawrence Pierce, and James Guthrie, *Re-Inventing Public Education: How Contracting Can Transform America's Schools* (University of Chicago Press, 1997).

7. This corresponds to Phillip Schlechty's conception of the principal as a leader of leaders. See Phillip Schlechty, *Schools for the 21st Century* (Jossey-Bass Publishers, 1990).

8. For an account of how New York City central office demands on the principals of new schools eliminated opportunities for within-school leadership, see

Linda Darling-Hammond, Jacqueline Ancess, Kemly MacGregor, and David Zuckerman, "The Coalition Campus Project: Inching Toward Systemic Reform in New York City," unpublished manuscript, Columbia Teachers' College, 1994.

9. In the early 1990s, some schools in Montgomery County, Maryland, opted out of the district's "site-based management" program on grounds that it had decreased their freedom of action and increased district-mandated paperwork.

10. In Chicago, New York, and Detroit, for example, the principal does not have the keys to the school building. The building may be used when the custodian is there to unlock it. This gravely limits a principal's ability to use a school building as a community gathering place or to create new learning opportunities for students and their families. The rule that so limits principals is purely a result of collective bargaining, rather than a considered judgment that the school is not a safe place without a custodian present.

11. Stepping into this vacuum recently, Lauren Resnick and her colleagues at the Learning Research and Development Center at the University of Pittsburgh have developed an aggressive effort to help principals become leaders of learning.

12. See Steve Farkas and Jean Johnson, *Different Drummers: How Teachers of Teachers View Public Education* (New York: Public Agenda Foundation, 1998).

13. A former district human resources director in Seattle reports that the district, while suffering a severe shortage of principals, received applications from twenty-four experienced heads of nonprofit human services organizations but was unable, under state certification rules, to hire any of them.

14. In the spring of 2002, amid heavy political overtones and parental demonstrations, a high school principal on Mercer Island, Washington, threatened to resign, claiming that working sixty or more hours a week was too much. He remained as coprincipal, essentially worrying about the day-to-day functioning of the school, while another coprincipal was hired to worry about curriculum.

15. Roza, *A Matter of Definition.*

16. Bradley Portin, Paul Schneider, Michael de Armond, and Lauren Gundlach, *Making Sense of Leading Schools: A Study of the School Principalship* (Seattle: Center on Reinventing Public Education, 2003).

17. *Is There a Shortage of Qualified Candidates for Openings in the Principalship?* (Arlington, Va.: National Association of Secondary School Principals, 1998).

18. Many of the Rand studies are reported only in classified publications. Two unclassified examples: Carl Builder, *The Army in the Strategic Planning Process: Who Shall Bell the Cat?* (Santa Monica: Rand, 1987); and Paul T. Hill, Thomas K. Glennon, and Susan J. Bodilly, *Termination of Air Force Activities* (Santa Monica: Rand, 1989).

19. For information, see www.houstonannenberg.org/initiatives.htm.

20. For a complete exposition of this point, see Paul T. Hill and Robin J. Lake, *Charter Schools and Accountability in Public Education* (Brookings, 2002), chap. 2.

21. Bradley Portin, *Explorations in Principal Leadership Across an Array of School Types*, paper prepared for presentation at the 2002 UCEA Convention, Cincinnati, 2002.

EIGHT   *Rethinking Data*
Capacity

MARGUERITE ROZA

MOST URBAN CITIES lack the strategic information
to successfully identify and implement a district reform strategy. Although
the term "data-driven decisionmaking" has become a popular idea in school
reform, urban districts do not have access to the right data to make the
best decisions.

That is not to say that districts do not have and use data, as is evidenced by the three-inch-thick binders of data handed to school board
members at each meeting. The most commonly reported data describe the
current conditions of schools, which often include average scores broken
down by subject area, socioeconomic status, minority group, poverty, education level of students' mothers, and so on. Information might also include attendance and dropout rates, disciplinary actions, and reams of
budget documents that list nearly every line item expenditure recorded by
the central office. Recently, states and districts have added accountability
data equipped with ratings that compare individual schools' scores with
other schools with similar demographics. While voluminous and often
important, these data do not inform leaders faced with having to make
strategic decisions to improve their system.

Rather than more descriptive data or even accountability data, districts now need to build a local analysis capacity that enables them to
collect and utilize data for strategic planning and monitoring. As this chapter demonstrates, such a capacity needs to:

—Inform the strategic decisions that affect students;

83

—Track the availability of key resources and their connection to student outcomes;

—Provide early warnings of improvement or decline, school by school; and

—Provide a districtwide capacity profile that enables leaders to focus their strategy.

This chapter highlights these four key features of a local analysis capacity, discusses some of the challenges that districts meet in trying to gain this information, and demonstrates how and why an independent institution would be most suited to meet this need.

Inform the Strategic Decisions That Affect Students

Reform is now becoming high stakes. District leaders no longer have the luxury of continuing with business as usual or tweaking existing programs to make minor changes. Many urban superintendents and principals must show real results in the short term. But what are their options, and how do they know for sure what decisions will affect the bottom line—student performance?

Paradoxically, current leaders get little help from the wave of performance data created as part of accountability programs or from the school and district report cards that are supposed to be used for this purpose. Many districts and thirty-six states collect data for "school report cards," although these report cards generally do not provide the kind of information that leaders can use to improve their schools. One researcher, Russell French, has examined the data in these report cards: "One of the things that struck us most was that so many of the things that are reported have so little to do with student outcomes."[1] In his research, he found that, in many cases, what is reported is simply what is available or what is required by law, and that there is very little information that would offer insights into the factors that could contribute to varying performance levels.[2] And while accountability data that profile performance by school, grade, and subject do highlight successes and trouble areas, such data do not clarify choices among options for leaders. "I need data that tell me what to do," pleads one superintendent at a data workshop.

The more relevant data this superintendent seeks reveal the links between feasible actions for leaders and the real results for students. An example

Figure 8-1. *Average Student Performance in Three Programs, New York*

Percent

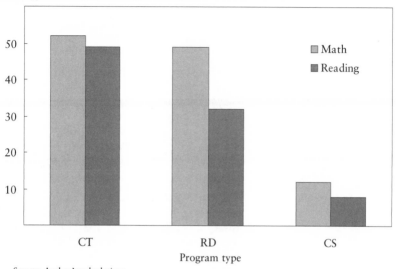

Source: Author's calculations.

comes from an urban district in New York. Here a consultant was able to compare student performance in several different instructional programs designed for students with a specific type of disability (as shown in figure 8-1). The three programs, labeled CT, RD, and CTS, had evolved in different locations throughout the district and had never been examined for their impact on student performance.

With this type of data, the district was able to compare the impact each program was having on students with the programs' costs and feasibility. The district could then make a well-informed strategic decision to expand the CT and RD programs while eliminating CS.

In contrast, most leaders are faced with data that compare students' outcomes with factors over which school leaders have no control, such as the demographics of their student population. The data essentially cement assumptions about the capabilities of each school's students.

In contrast, strategic data should direct our attention close to the learning process, where decisions are more likely to have an impact. In another example, data from Tennessee show yearly growth for all students in the state, distinguishing children who stayed in one school, changed schools many times, or changed schools only when they had completed all the grades available in their original school (figure 8-2). Researchers, in ana-

Figure 8-2. *Mean Student Gains as a Result of District Policy, Tennessee*
Percent

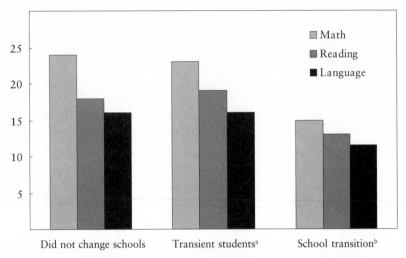

Source: Based on data from William Sanders, Arnold Saxton, and others, "Effects of Building Change on Indicators of Student Academic Growth," *Evaluation Perspectives*, 1994, p. 3.

a. Students who entered a new school at any grade other than the lowest grade offered.

b. Students making a scheduled transition, that is, entering a different school at the lowest grade offered.

lyzing the database, found that, on average, students learned less in the years they were making the scheduled transition from elementary to middle school and from middle to high school. Interestingly, the "transient" students who relocated outside of these scheduled transition years did not suffer, as many educators had long suspected would be true, indicating that the problem was more about the schooling than the disruption to the student. This kind of data, if used correctly, might point to options for fewer scheduled transitions or other efforts directed at reducing the number of times students must change schools.

To uncover this sort of powerfully strategic data, an analysis must start with variables that are close to the learning process. For instance, the analysis might investigate how and what students are taught and the impact of different strategies, programs, and experiences on groups of students. With this information, leaders can zero in on programs or policies that are most likely to have a real impact on students.

Track the Availability of Key Resources

Education is a labor-intense enterprise that relies fundamentally on its human resource capacity. Understanding this capacity is a critical precursor to developing an effective and powerful reform strategy. However, districts rarely rely on human resources data to drive policy decisions because they do not systematically collect information on this basic input. Similarly, while districts tend to track categories of expenditures (staffing, administrative, and so on), they have only limited data about the relative value of investments for certain students and specific programs. These are the core inputs and should drive decisions about how limited resources are utilized to maximize their effectiveness.

For forty years, educators have accepted that poverty is the most important variable in determining achievement. Research now emerging from a decade's worth of data on student achievement in Tennessee indicates that teachers' effectiveness trumps all other factors. Studies from Dallas and Boston, which have used a reliable system to measure teachers' effectiveness and student performance, now confirm the Tennessee data: students placed with one or more bad teachers emerge a full year behind their peers who are taught by a highly effective teacher.[3] After three years in a row of poor teachers, the effects on students are catastrophic. Many of these children never recover.

While many districts are reluctant to "evaluate" their teachers based on student performance, this information is critical for a host of strategic decisions. First, it gives the district a glimpse of how many highly and least effective teachers are currently in their schools. Not surprisingly, the percentage of ineffective and effective teachers is not evenly distributed among schools or districts. Highly effective schools typically have higher percentages of more effective teachers.

Gathering data on these indicators can help district leaders determine if their worst schools are plagued by disproportionately high percentages of least effective teachers, or if the entire district is struggling with inadequate teachers. These kinds of findings can point to the need for better teachers across the board or only in selected schools or programs. Effectiveness can be correlated with certain hiring characteristics, enabling districts to zero in on their best sources for teachers. Longitudinal data can reveal the effects of various professional development efforts. Most important, districts can learn from their best teachers. In Minneapolis, the district surveyed the best second grade reading teachers and found that they spend more time on oral and independent reading—a strategy that was then shared among other teachers.

Many successful schools have principals who admit to spending a great deal of time evaluating their staff, selecting the best new teachers, and coaching poor teachers out of the school. Having the information to employ a human resources strategy at the district level can be an extremely powerful route to reform. In an encouraging example, New York's Community District Two was transformed from a struggling district to one that has received national attention for significantly improving student performance. Several prominent researchers following the effort attributed much of the progress to a systematic and persistent human resources effort. Under the leadership of Anthony Alvarado, a select cadre of talented leaders spent much of their time working directly with teachers and principals. Over the years, these leaders are said to have gradually "counseled out" the least effective teachers and hand-selected their replacements. As a result, the district slowly but systematically built a much more talented teaching staff than it did ten years earlier. The human resources data described in this section enable district leaders to have access on a broad scale to information that currently only the more astute principals and district leaders use.

But the data on human resources should not start and stop with effectiveness data. Districts need to track the supply of teachers and principals, and much of the data are readily collectable for those who are interested. For instance, by calling around to a few schools in Los Angeles, we found that for each open position, low-income schools like Gompers Middle School and Grape Elementary receive one to three applicants at best. In contrast, Westwood Elementary, in a higher-income neighborhood, receives approximately 130 applicants for each position, virtually guaranteeing that this school's teachers are the cream of the crop. While most districts have no clear policy for addressing the distribution of teachers within the district, certainly leaving it to individual teachers' preferences about where to apply for jobs makes it nearly impossible for struggling schools to bring in talent. Typically districts wait until there is an impending threat of classes without teachers before they gather any real human resources data.

And with all the ivory tower research on the importance of effective school leadership, districts are still slow to monitor even basic indicators on their own supply of principals. In Philadelphia, where one struggling school had six principals in six years, the district still does not record turnover.

One of the reasons that districts have been able to ignore some of the critical variables is that current accounting schemes hide the implications of their human resources decisions. For example, in many districts, "aver-

Figure 8-3. *Impact of Budgeting Scheme, Seattle*

Per pupul allocation (dollars)

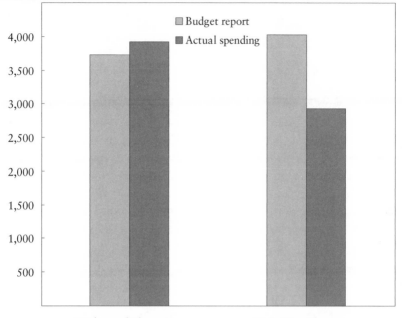

Wedgwood Elementary   M. L. King Elementary

age teacher costing" is used to account for money spent on human resources. Districts use a fixed average salary to compute teacher costs for
school-by-school budget reports. The district then pays out the real salaries—salaries that are not fixed but vary substantially with experience
and other qualifications. So, in reality, schools with less qualified (and
less expensive) teachers subsidize those with better (and generally more
costly) teachers.

An analysis of the real data shows the impact of this budgeting scheme
in Seattle. Personnel funds designated for schools with larger numbers of
poor and minority students—schools that consistently operate with less
expensive teachers—are essentially used to pay for the costly teachers in
the high-rent north end at schools like Wedgwood (figure 8-3). Schools
like M. L. King Elementary, which cannot attract the most expensive teachers, are cheated out of about $300,000 a year—resources that could go
toward hiring better teachers, lowering class sizes, or supporting other
efforts that might benefit the students.

In the Seattle schools, it is obvious that the district's budget accounting system systematically masks differences in real school resources in such a way that favors the better schools. Houston has taken a bold move toward removing this policy, requiring schools to hire teachers within their budget constraints. Schools that cannot hire more experienced staff will keep the extra money. Most important, the district now accurately records how much it spends on each school, and for each type of student, and can track these relative investments against desired outcomes.

This strategy comes directly from the understanding that all educational inputs are "costs" that imply trade-offs. The reality is that in the absence of accurate expenditure data, districts have been slow to address these critical inputs, instead favoring curriculum changes, add-on programs, and even the latest wave of standards-based reforms. Clearly, accurate school and student-based expenditure analysis is the first step toward strategic decisions that maximize outputs with fixed inputs.

Provide Early Warnings of Improvement or Decline, School by School

Picture the scenario: a new superintendent takes the helm of an urban district with more than one hundred schools (as is the case every two to three years in most big-city districts). Many of these schools differ significantly in their access to real resources, capacity to educate children, and, most important, current potential for success. In rethinking the types of analysis that would assist these superintendents, it is clear that districts need mechanisms for quickly assessing and communicating where each school is on its current trajectory.

Consider a struggling school that starts with a complex student population. Substandard performance gives the school a bad reputation. The best teachers (and principals) choose to work elsewhere, and the school experiences ever-escalating staff turnover. High turnover takes its toll as parents have few relationships with school staff, programs lack coherency, and the faculty is perpetually inexperienced. The school's reputation continues to dive, and parents with choices take their children elsewhere.

Although it is possible to break the cycle, in most cases, the longer the school has been going down this path, the more difficult it is to recover. Unfortunately, in urban districts with as many as a hundred schools, superintendents (often new to their position) are unlikely to recognize the subtle signs of a downward spiral and instead wait for poor scores before taking real action. In fact, schools typically start out on this downward spiral long before they get labeled a "focus school" or a "school under review" or an "opportunity school" or any of the other euphemisms used to describe years of educational failure.

Yet early warning signs are not hard to find. Principals, teachers, and parents recognize growing enthusiasm or mounting frustration before it shows up in scores. Aggregated data on these perceptions can be seen in the number of staff members requesting a transfer, changes in the percentages of students that apply to private schools, or even staff and parent surveys on perceptions of the school's focus or quality of leadership.

In Seattle where students can list their preferences for any one of the district's ten high schools, these preferences speak volumes. In 1999, 620 students listed Roosevelt High School as their first choice, whereas only 94 students listed Ranier Beach High School as their first choice. In many ways, these numbers serve as a consolidated measure of many complicated and interrelated factors, such as school climate, student performance, principal's leadership, quality of teachers, program offerings, and progress over time.

In truth, very few districts use such revealing measures. So in large urban cities with many schools, it is especially difficult to sift through the descriptive data and get a quick, accurate picture of where each school is headed. Yet in some ways the districts serve as a conglomeration of many different schools with varying needs, so this information is vital to managing the district.

At one education forum, we presented several local school profiles created from a few relevant and available indicators to demonstrate the power of this kind of consolidated information. One of the schools was a "Red Flag School," depicted in table 8-1, a high school previously deemed average but now experiencing declining achievement scores, growing staff dissatisfaction, and waning student interest in the school (in a district with a high level of choice at the secondary school level). Another was a "School on the Rise." This was also a high school, with nearly average achievement results over the years, but recently its scores had been improving. The school had a stable faculty that gave high marks for climate and leadership, and it was becoming more frequently selected by families as a first-choice placement.

While all of the indicators used in these profiles are generally available in that district, school leaders are rarely faced with reports that forecast

Table 8-1. *Portraits of Two Types of Schools*

Red Flag School	School on the Rise
Scores just below average but declining in each of the last three years	Scores near average but increasing
Declining numbers of students designating this school as their first choice	Increasing number of students designating this school as their first choice
5 to 10 applicants per teacher opening	20 applicants per teacher opening
Declining marks by staff for climate, leadership, and team cohesion	High marks by staff for leadership and team cohesion
More per pupil resources than the district's average	Roughly average per pupil expenditures for this district

Source: University of Washington, Policy Makers Exchange, April 2001.

whether schools are on the rise or decline. As a result, district leaders from this district had difficulty recognizing their own school profiles. Equally fascinating was that even principals with access to this very information from the district were unsure how their schools would stack up on this kind of profile.

And yet the applications of this kind of consolidated information are clear. On the one hand, district leaders can identify early on when schools are in serious trouble and act accordingly. On the other hand, a district can recognize when schools, even those with lagging scores, are likely to improve over the coming years and will not benefit from serious upheaval.

Provide a Districtwide Capacity Profile

These kinds of school-by-school profiles could then be one part of a districtwide profile highlighting the performance and capacities of the total organization. Like other effective enterprises, districts should shape strategic decisions with information on availability of key resources, the utilization of their current capacities, and the progress on current efforts. In education terms, districts need to look at things like the variations in school quality throughout the district, the ability to hire and retain good teachers and principals, the forecasts for future retirements and staffing, and the cost of trade-offs of current programs and other options available in their region. A strategy based on this information is much more likely to be successful in both the short term and the long term.

Consider, for example, a district where the capacity profile reveals broad human resources needs throughout the district with few teacher applicants, forecasts for many retirements, and higher-than-normal rates of "inadequate" teachers. This is a district where scores are low in almost every school, especially in comparison to surrounding districts not suffering the same critical human resources issues. Years of add-on professional development efforts have left the district with numerous teacher training efforts operating simultaneously.

In this district, the data point to a large-scale, districtwide human resources effort involving recruiting and hiring better teachers for all schools. With what appears to be an adequate supply of teaching talent in the local region (as evidenced by comparisons to other local districts), this district needs to get more proactive in ensuring that it has access to some of that talent. The district might think about working with the local university to encourage placement of more student teachers in the district schools while training principals on how to mentor and retain this aspiring source of talent. At the same time the district might consolidate its professional development to provide a more coherent plan for improving teacher performance.

In contrast, consider a district where the districtwide analysis shows mixed performance, with some schools doing well and others in a downward spiral. Comparisons among schools show that some schools in the district are having no problems recruiting teachers while others operate with fewer real dollars, higher teacher turnover, and less stability among principals.

This kind of profile should dictate a very different strategy than for the previous district. First, district leaders might consider a more targeted reform strategy that addresses specific schools, while not disrupting the successful schools. For example, schoolwide reforms could be mandated for selected buildings or incentives provided for the best principals to stay in struggling schools. At the same time, the district might look for ways to draw better teachers to where they are needed most, perhaps by more evenly distributing the real resources among schools.

In any case, the strategy should reflect the district's current dynamics, capacities, and needs. Then, as districts experience transitions in leadership (when superintendents, school board members, and other leaders move on), the district profile is there to create staying power for the ongoing strategy.

Finally, the districtwide profile can help leaders monitor their strategies. By methodically examining each step of the process that motivated the strategy, this kind of data can provide real evidence of progress in the short term.

Chicago serves as one of the best large-scale examples of using data effectively to monitor an effort. In 1988 Illinois enacted a law, Public Act 85-1418, implementing a decentralizing plan to combat years of well-publicized school failure. The site-based leadership structure included local school councils empowered with such responsibilities as hiring and firing the principal and creating each school's improvement plan. This strategy used a logic model that assumed that "democratic participation . . . [would] leverage systemic organizational changes [in schools] that [would in turn] focus attention on instructional improvement."[4] Instructional improvement would then directly affect student achievement.

At the same time as the strategy was implemented, a team of researchers, predominantly from the University of Chicago, was tasked with monitoring and evaluating the effectiveness of the reform. These researchers developed indicators designed to evaluate each step in the reform implementation.

For example, to find out whether or not organizational change was taking place, the researchers examined parental engagement, the school's access to new ideas, the professional community, the locus of responsibility for change, and participation in strategic planning. The team was then able to measure the organizational change in each school. These kinds of sophisticated benchmark indicators not only are useful to the district leaders trying to monitor the progress of their efforts but also help school leaders and teachers track their own progress.

The consequences of *not* monitoring a strategy can be exemplified in an effort to recruit more teachers for Los Angeles. As precipitated by state-mandated reductions in class size and a high teacher turnover, the Los Angeles Unified School District launched a campaign to recruit new teachers. During several months of this campaign, interested applicants could not get through to the personnel office using the district's main hiring phone number. As one personnel official interviewed for this study explained, the district did not "have adequate staff to man that phone line in the summer." One can only imagine how many potential candidates are now working in surrounding districts as a result of this small oversight.

In sum, a districtwide profile should inform leaders about current problems and their causes, provide information on real options, and monitor progress toward existing efforts. But most important, a useful analysis synthesizes and highlights the most relevant information, providing leaders with a clear rationale for selecting an appropriate strategy.

Why It's So Hard for Districts

In truth, very few districts currently collect and use the kinds of data profiled in this chapter. Most of the examples presented were assembled by researchers and consultants external to the districts they analyze. In fact, it is unlikely that most districts will ever have the capacity to perform these analyses that are so critically needed for their own reform.

In the 1970s and early 1980s, many larger districts had research departments tasked with analyzing data. However, as school resources were tightened, research departments were scaled back so much that most in-house data experts now spend most of their time reporting data on a few descriptive indicators, many of which are required by law. There are, of course, pockets of valuable analysis—one example being Los Angeles's recent tracking and reporting of teachers' experience across schools. This practice, however, exists as a result of the *Rodriguez* v. *LAUSD* consent decree ordering the district to take steps to achieve more equitable distribution of teachers.[5] With so many immediate needs in the forefront of district operations, much district leadership becomes reactionary, and the planning and investment necessary for good data analysis do not get done.

But even if districts were to reinstate their research departments and direct them to obtain the important information, it is unlikely that an in-house administrative unit would ever be able to perform and report this kind of analysis in any comprehensive manner. First, within-district units are not impartial to other parts of the organization, and maintaining this neutrality is critical. When so many district decisions are clouded in district politics, the reporting authority must stay steadfast and neutral and transcend changes in district leadership. Imagine if the superintendent asked the research department to confirm that his or her most recent strategy is working.

Second, this kind of analysis requires that district employees handle data on sensitive topics such as teachers' effectiveness. Many districts are loath to collect these data, knowing that once collected they are then public record. If parents knew exactly how each teacher was performing compared with all other teachers, many would fight to have their children placed with the best ones, creating a potentially difficult situation for the district. In one attempt by this author to obtain public information on school-level spending disparities, a budget official balked at uncovering such information, admitting that the data would surely force changes in allocations, and she had no time to make these changes. Some states, in fact, have avoided collecting student-level data because of their concern about maintaining students' privacy rights.

Finally, good information requires technological capacity and expert analysis by those that understand broad issues in education. In the recent past, collecting and integrating classroom and student-level data were expensive and time consuming. With vast improvements in electronic data management, many more opportunities for analysis now exist. District leaders have been slow to respond in part because warehousing and analysis expertise is difficult to create and sustain for most districts. Although some companies have recognized the need for data analysis capacity in education and have even produced data warehousing software and services, many district leaders acknowledge that their challenge is finding the time and expertise to understand what the data tell them.

In an early model of this kind of new institution, the Washington State Information Processing Cooperative (WSIPC) operates seventeen data centers across Washington state. Those seventeen data centers provide data warehousing and some analysis software to 280 of the 296 school districts in the state of Washington. According to the state superintendent of education's office, users of the cooperative lower their information system costs by more than 50 percent. For data warehousing, the demand is clear. The next step for these kinds of institutions is the more critical role of providing the key analysis necessary for strategic decisionmaking.

Districts Should Rely on Outside Institutions for Analysis

A better option is for external organizations to perform this analysis for districts. The idea is not new, nor is it unique to education. Currently, university researchers do some work in this area, which mostly amounts to bits of analysis on isolated topics. Some professional consulting and accounting companies have also dabbled in school district analysis, with few long-term relationships—in part as a result of the very high costs of the arrangement. Private industry has for years relied on outside market research firms, accountants, and management consultants to clarify trends, identify new business options, provide due diligence services, and generally inform strategic decisionmaking.

What is needed is an external organization primarily tasked with managing districts' data and serving as their primary source of analysis. The independent, nonprofit, or university-based organization could provide this service for many districts, efficiently capitalizing on the economies of scale. By managing the data for multiple districts, the organization can maintain a technologically advanced hardware and software system that would never stay current in a school district. The organization would then have the capacity to serve the uneven demands of each district while sustaining the expertise necessary for effective analysis. The organization's professionals would conduct the analysis, understand the field of education and the particular demands and needs of the region, perfect indicators that can be appropriate for many districts, and synthesize and communicate findings to top education leaders. The leaders can use their time effectively as decisionmakers instead of trying to be data experts.

As an organization outside of the district, analysis should remain impartial and accurate. If the actual data were housed at the external organization, then only findings communicated to the district would become public information. So, for instance, if the district wanted information about the distribution of effective teachers among schools, it could get that information without having to divulge each teacher's exact level of effectiveness. Finally, managing the data in a single location with experts trained in confidentiality could ensure proper control over the database.

In sum, the outside organization would maintain the data system and provide critical analyses necessary to make the district's strategic decisions. An outside organization provides the best option for attaining a financially feasible, technologically efficient, impartial, and informed data analysis capacity.

Notes

1. Lynn Olson, "Report Cards for Schools," *Education Week, Quality Counts,* vol. 18, no. 27 (Editorial Projects in Education, 1999), p. 27.

2. Russell French and Gordon Bobbett, "A Detailed Analysis of Report Cards on Schools Produced in Eight Eastern States and a Synthesis of Report Card Studies in Nineteen States," paper presented to the American Educational Research Association, San Francisco, 1995.

3. William Sanders and June Rivers, *Cumulative and Residual Effects of Teachers on Future Student Academic Achievement,* Research Progress Report (University of Tennessee Value-Added Research and Assessment Center, 1996).

4. Anthony Bryk, Penny Bender Bebring, David Kerbow, Sharon Rollow, and John Easton, *Charting Chicago School Reform: Democratic Localism as a Lever for Change* (Harper Collins, 1999).

5. Stuart Biegel and Julie Slayton, *Policy Issues and Prospects: Access to Equal Educational Opportunity* (University of California, Los Angeles, 1997).

NINE   *A School*

Inspectorate

JAMES HARVEY

THE LANGUAGE OF the British School Inspections Act of 1996 rolls impressively off the page: "Be it enacted by the Queen's most Excellent Majesty, by and with the advice and consent of the Lords Spiritual and Temporal, and Commons, in this present Parliament assembled, and by the authority of the same, as follows. . . ."[1]

With that stock formulation, developed over centuries to precede every enactment of Parliament, the English government in 1997 rechartered Her Majesty's Inspectorate of Schools in England and Wales, a system first established in 1839.[2] The legislation defined the functions and authority of separate chief inspectors for each country, provided for a registry of inspectors, outlined a procedure for inspections and the reports they produced, and defined powers over schools "requiring special measures." Separately, as part of the Labor Government's devolution of authority, similar Scottish statutes provided in 2001 for Her Majesty's Inspectorate of Education in Scotland.[3]

These institutions are part of a great tradition of inspectorates in British civil administration, dating back more than a century. These include Her Majesty's Inspectors of Constabulary, Her Majesty's Chief Inspector of Prisons, Her Majesty's Fire Service Inspectorate, Her Majesty's Railway Inspectorate, and Her Majesty's Inspectorate of Pollution, among others.[4] The scope of issues before these officials is as broad as the range of institutions they are required to evaluate.

If imitation is the greatest form of flattery, then Her Majesty's Inspectorate of Schools can be said to be fawned upon. In 1995, the school reform enacted in Massachusetts provided for a system of school inspectors for the charter schools the reform authorized.[5] Denmark and Israel have adapted inspectorates partially copied from the English model. The Republic of Ireland began to experiment with a system of inspectors in 1998–99.[6] Apparently, considerable interest exists in on-site, human, face-to-face evaluation as part of comprehensive assessment of school effectiveness.

Naturally, several questions arise. Could something similar to these English inspectors usefully be added to the American reform movement? Might site visits supplement the test-based accountability approach that now dominates American schools? Can we improve the emphases on standards and evaluation embedded in American school reform by borrowing anything from the inspectorate system in England? Or is the concept of the inspectorate valueless in today's reform context—as dated, timeworn, and anachronistic as the enabling language of English statutes, the idea of "Lords Spiritual and Temporal," and the very concept of "Majesty," indeed monarchy, itself?

In sum, my view is that although the concept cannot be imported root and branch from the Old World to the New, experiments in Kentucky, Massachusetts, and Virginia clearly show that expert assistance to distressed schools provides many of the benefits of an inspectorate without much of the baggage.

Power and Authority of the Inspectorate

The power and authority of the chief inspector of schools, and consequently the derivative powers enjoyed by school inspectors, are sweeping. Unlike the inspector-general of the U.S. Department of Education, who is empowered to investigate only programs and procedures supported by the parent department, the chief inspectors are authorized to look into the nooks and crannies of practically every state-funded primary and secondary school in England, Scotland, and Wales.

The Office for Standards in Education (OFSTED), officially the Office of Her Majesty's Chief Inspector of Schools in England, is a nonministerial government department, independent of the cabinet's Department of Education and Skills.[7] It is charged with improving "standards of achievement and quality of education through regular independent inspection [of schools], public reporting and informed independent advice."[8] It defines its principal task as managing a system of school inspection that provides for regular examination of all 24,000 schools in England that are wholly or mainly state supported. In recent years, the office's writ has been expanded to include reviews of local education authorities; initial teacher training courses; private, voluntary, and independent nursery programs; independent schools; service children's education; and youth services funded by the local education authority.

In pursuit of this broad mandate, the chief inspector possesses statutory authority to keep the secretary of state for education and employment informed about:

—The quality of education provided by schools in England;

—The educational standards achieved by pupils in those schools;

—Whether the financial resources made available to those schools are managed efficiently; and

—The spiritual, moral, social, and cultural development of pupils at those schools.

The legislation gives the chief inspector the right to enter the premises of any school under inspection and the right to inspect and make copies of any records or other documents kept by the school. Any school employee willfully obstructing the chief inspector in the exercise of these functions is liable for summary conviction and an administrative fine. These authorities (and the accompanying civil penalties) are specifically extended to registered inspectors operating under the direction of the chief inspector.

Scale and Scope

In England and Wales, the chief inspectors oversee a large system designed to ensure that every state school is inspected every six years. In Scotland, the goal is to ensure a "generational cycle" of school inspection, so that parents can expect to receive an inspection report for both the primary and secondary schools their children attend.[9] What this has meant, in England, is that in the years from 1996 to 2001, between 4,160 and 7,286 schools were inspected each year, with the largest number inspected in the first year. After that, inspections stabilized annually at 4,100 to 4,700 schools.[10] In Scotland, Her Majesty's educational watchdog looked into more than 600 schools between 1998 and 2001.[11] In both countries, primary school inspections annually outnumbered those in secondary schools by rates of four or five to one.

The definition of an "inspector" can be deceptive. The chief inspector is responsible for both Her Majesty's inspectors and for establishing and maintaining a system for the regular inspection of schools by *independent* inspectors. This obligation requires OFSTED to arrange for the training of independent inspectors, keep a register of people approved to conduct inspections, maintain a separate roll of people who have been approved to work as *members* of inspection teams, and keep the inspection system under review. Inspections are conducted under contract, and OFSTED maintains that important distinctions exist between these registered contract inspectors and ones designated as "Her Majesty's inspectors." One of the critical distinctions is that HMIs are employed by OFSTED, and registered inspectors are not. Registered inspectors are contract employees of the agency.

Another critical distinction is that the registered inspectors, not Her Majesty's inspectors, carry out the evaluations. Her Majesty's inspectors monitor the process, assess the work of the registered inspectors and their teams, and provide feedback on their strengths and weaknesses. Where inspection teams indicate that schools require special measures because they are failing or likely to fail, Her Majesty's inspectors must corroborate that judgment. They must then assess the progress of schools in that position, visiting each of them within five to seven months of their first inspection and "subsequently until they are judged ready to be taken out of that category."[12]

OFSTED considers four major categories of independent inspector significant.[13] "Registered inspectors" conduct the inspection of a school and carry the responsibility, under law, to conduct, select, and deploy the inspection team and develop the report. "Team inspectors" inspect particular aspects of the school (for example, the curriculum or school management) and contribute to the report. "Lay inspectors" are parents or citizens "who have no personal experience of any significance in the management of any school or the provision of education in any school." And "registered nursery inspectors" conduct the inspection of funded nursery programs (without the assistance of a team). The Scottish system employs similar categories—inspectors, "associate inspectors" with experience in a relevant field (a practicing teacher, head teacher, or education service officer), and lay members.

The Process

The process is not a simple one. In Scotland, at both the primary and secondary levels, a team of five to six members (two to three inspectors, the lay member, and possibly an associate assessor) will carry out the inspection. Schools are typically given about three weeks' notice of the pending inspection. Generally, Scottish inspectors are interested in answering three key questions: How effective is the school? How well are the pupils performing? How well is the school managed? To answer these questions, inspectors will look at educational programs, pupil support, students' personal and social development, arrangements for child protection, and important aspects of school management.

For primary schools in Scotland, the inspection visit takes a full week, with a visit to the school ahead of time by the reporting officer to discuss the details of the upcoming visit. At the secondary level, the Scottish process seems even more detailed. It is carried out in two phases, each lasting four days. The first four days seem to be mainly preparatory.[14] During that time, staff, parents, students, and the school's board of governors are informed of the purposes of the inspection. And staff may attend a briefing about the inspection. During this phase, questionnaires are issued to all staff and parents and to a sample of students.

During the second phase, a follow-up to all the issues identified during phase 1 (from the profile provided by the board and from an analysis of the returned questionnaires) will be completed. Staff and students will be interviewed and classrooms visited. The inspectors will look into how provision is made for the personal and social development of students, and classroom visits will explicitly explore the learning ethos. Child protection features of the school will be examined, including determining how the school responds to allegations or complaints against staff members. Finally, the inspectors will look into the quality of school management and leadership in relationship to the care and welfare of students and the school development plan.

The lay members of the inspection teams are explicitly invited to examine how the school and its students interact with parents and the local community. They help ensure that the views of parents and students are taken into account during the inspection. Schools are provided with a debriefing after the inspection and can normally expect a written report within five to six weeks of the visit. Following discussions with the school leadership, the report is normally published and sent to all parents several weeks later.

Clearly this is a labor-intensive process, and the results are much more detailed and nuanced than is typically available from a review of standardized test scores. Although student achievement results feature prominently in the evaluations, and are used as a gauge of progress in the national compilations of inspected schools, the inspections cover in detail many aspects of school performance. How well are students taught? Is the teachers' planning effective? What about teachers' expectations? How well do students achieve? How do the students behave in school? What does attendance look like? Is the appropriate *statutory* curriculum in place? How well is the school led and managed? How effective is the governing board? Are resources used strategically? Has the school improved since the last inspection? On dozens of questions such as these, OFSTED produces national data indicating the proportion of schools that are deemed excellent or very good, good, satisfactory, or poor.

Major Elements

Clearly, the inspectorate system is not a quick snapshot of student performance in the school. Most inspectors are veteran teachers or administrators. The inspection itself, in the words of Thomas A. Wilson, is a "practitioner's way of seeing, thinking about, and discussing school value. . . . Inspection has evolved as a methodology of practitioners, not as a social science methodology. What inspectors consider important, how they decide what is true, how they value goodness and excellence, and how they carry out their day-to-day work—all vary in interesting ways from the usual American approach to evaluating schools."[15]

The knowledge developed during inspections, says Wilson, "has value to policymakers, to those who seek ways to help the school, and, most important, to those at the school itself."

Wilson believes that several major elements are at the heart of the success of the inspection system:

—Being There. No element is more central to inspection than visiting a school while it is in session to view what students, teachers, staff, and parents are doing and to gain a sense of what they think they are accomplishing.

—Focus. The focus of inspections has changed over time, circling around key issues: the school, achievement, the classroom, the curriculum, and teaching and learning. More recently inspections have focused on students' test performance.

—Judgment. The judgment of individual inspectors, and of the collective inspection team, is a key element of the process.

—Evidence. In support of judgments, evidence must be clear, precise, and accurate. Evidence may take shape around implementation of the national curriculum or standards for student work. It is collected by observing behavior—talking with students, interviewing teachers, and watching classes in action.

—Standards. Three kinds of standards are called on: the inspector's experience as a teacher or administrator, the inspector's current practice as an inspector, and public sources, including examination boards and national curriculum standards.

—Moderation of Individual Judgment. Moderation hones the judgment of individual inspectors into a team judgment. It is encouraged by a tradition of "thorough, open, rigorous team discussion" under the reporting inspector's leadership.

—Feedback to Teachers and Schools. An immediate debriefing for school staff is almost always a part of the inspection process.

—Inspection Report. Since 1983 all reports have been public documents in England, available to anyone requesting them. "Currently," says Wilson, "the published report of a school inspection is accepted as an authoritative and final statement about the quality of the school at the time of the inspection."

—School Follow-Up. School follow-up is what the school does with the results of the inspection. This is the school's responsibility, and government policy has recently required the boards of inspected schools to prepare an action plan on how they intend to respond.

—Government Policy. Reporting to government has always been a central purpose of all this activity. An annual report from the chief inspector, based on all reports for the year, provides summary statements about educational strengths and weaknesses and outlines potential areas for response.[16]

In all of this work, understanding how well the schools *provide* for students is the heart of the matter. *Provision,* says Wilson, revolves around teaching and learning; it is tangible because "an inspector can see and comment on it. He or she does not need to infer its presence from a component of the school, such as school climate, curriculum, or the number of books in the school library." The construct is similar, reports Wilson, to what Americans mean when they say that "parents provide well for their children." It includes a great deal more than material comfort: "When the English think about how well a school provides for its students, they think less in terms of inputs and outputs and more about all that happens at a school. Provision does not separate student performance from what a school provides. How students perform and how a school adjusts its provision in light of that performance are integral parts of provision."[17]

The Commitment

This century-and-a-half-old system of school inspections is a massive commitment of time, energy, resources, and human capital. Although data on the number of inspectors are hard to come by, if we assume that a five-member team visited each of the 4,100-odd schools inspected in 2001 and that each team spent an average of fifteen days preparing for the visit, participating in the visit, writing up the results, and following up, some sense of the scope of the effort can be imagined. Assume for the sake of argument that each team could complete ten schools during a nine-month school year. Four hundred and ten teams of five people apiece would be required to examine all 4,100 schools, that is to say, more than 2,000 inspectors of various kinds.

Certainly the number of individuals needed would be significantly higher than that, perhaps twice as high or more. It is unlikely that any team could complete ten inspections without collapsing. Moreover, team composition changes from school to school as different expertise is sought and individuals' schedules are taken into account. A minimum of 4,000 inspectors available is not out of the question. In fact, when OFSTED added preschool programs to its writ, the chief inspector's office found itself with 1,800 new childcare inspectors on its books.[18]

Quite apart from the commitment in resources and personnel, the "inspectorate" system represents a commitment to live, on-the-ground evaluation of school quality, conducted by practitioners and lay people. This is quite a different concept from the American social-science-driven commitment to numbers as a basis for judgments about schools. Since the 1990s began, English policymakers have paid more attention to numbers as well, especially to indicators of student achievement. But they are equally interested in informed assessments of student and parental satisfaction, quality of teachers, and effectiveness of school management and board leadership. As understood by this system of inspectors, there is nothing simple about the bottom line of school effectiveness.

As Wilson puts it, "When the English want to know whether a school is good or not, they send an inspector to visit it."[19]

Standards and Accreditation: American Analogs

In the United States, although nothing comparable to this vast system of inspectors exists, two analogs can be identified. The first is the emphasis in recent decades on standards-based reform. This reform agenda, driven by governors and business leaders, emphasizes the development of curriculum standards in half-a-dozen or more major curricular areas, along with related performance standards, cross-indexed with curriculum, for students at various age and grade levels (for example, performance standards in English and mathematics at the fourth-, seventh-, and twelfth-grade levels).

Once the standards have been developed, the standards-based reform movement then pushes for alignment of teacher training, curriculum, and assessment with the standards.

The second analog, school accreditation, is deceptively similar to the inspectorate system, since it involves school visits by teams of experts. The great accomplishment of accreditation has been to help American institutions distinguish secondary school offerings from undergraduate programs. (At the beginning of the twentieth century, many "colleges" were little more than preparatory schools.) Accreditation has also helped schools and colleges and universities improve themselves through periodic "reality checks" of their strengths and weaknesses. The general idea has been that the stamp of approval of a regional accrediting body signified that the school offered a satisfactory educational program.[20]

At its heart, accreditation is a collegial relationship in which peers help institutions assess and improve themselves. It relies heavily on school self-studies and peer reviews and site visits to confirm or invalidate these self-studies. In recent years, it has increasingly focused on issues of quality and student achievement. This entire process is designed to provide a warrant of school quality.

But although this accrediting system seems similar to the inspectorate approach, both it and the standards-based approach to assessment employed in the United States are quite different than the British system. Some of the major distinctions among the three approaches are outlined in table 9-1.

The most obvious broad distinctions to draw are that although both the inspectorate and standards-based reform rely on compulsion from the state and focus on results, accreditation, a regional and voluntary undertaking, relies more heavily on assessment of resources and process than it does on results. However, both the inspectorate and accreditation rely on complex and nuanced judgments about effectiveness, while standards-based reform, in the main, focuses on test scores, which proponents consider objective measures. Standards-based reform is disappointing in several

Table 9-1. *Key Features of Inspectorate, Accreditation, and Standards-Based Reform*

Item	Inspectorate	Accreditation	Standards-based reform
Locus of authority	National	Regional	State
Motivation	Compulsory	Voluntary	Compulsory
Results oriented?	Yes	No	Yes
Evaluation criteria	Complex and nuanced	Complex and nuanced	Test results
Parental/student views considered?	Yes	Yes	No
Finances considered?	Yes	Yes	No
Management examined	Yes	Yes	No
National assessment?	Yes	No	No
Time consuming?	Medium	High	Low
School self-study?	No	Yes	No
Expensive human capital?	Yes	No	No
Key elements			
Being there?	Yes	Yes	No
Focus?	Yes	Yes	Yes
Individual judgment?	Yes	Yes	No
Evidence	Yes	Yes	Yes
Standards	Yes	No	Yes
Team judgment	Yes	Yes	No
Immediate feedback	Yes	Normally	No
Public reports	Yes	No	Yes
School follow-up	Yes	Yes	Yes
Curriculum standards	Yes	No	Yes
Performance standards	Yes	No	Yes
Alignment	Yes	No	Yes

areas where the inspectorate and accreditation get high marks—particularly considering finances, school management, and the views of parents. Neither accreditation nor standards-based reform fares very well compared with the inspectorate on the timely issuance of reports. Accrediting teams are notorious for delaying their reports for months. And, in many states, assessments touted as helping schools identify student and school shortcomings are administered in the spring, with the results not available until the following school year, far too late to provide much help to anyone.

For key elements, such as on-site inspections, focus, public reports, and judgments about curriculum, neither accreditation nor test-based accountability performs as well as the inspectorate.

Table 9-2. *Strengths and Weaknesses of Inspectorate, Accreditation, and Standards-Based Reform*

	Inspectorate	Accreditation	Standards-based reform
Strengths	Hands on	Hands on	
	Practitioner based	Practitioner based	
	Examines individual schools	Examines individual schools	
	Comprehensive	Comprehensive	
	Standards based		Standards based
	Quantitative		Quantitative
	Qualitative	Qualitative	
	Identifies needed improvements	Identifies needed improvements	
	Warns public of schools in urgent need of improvement		Warns public of schools urgently needing improvement
Weaknesses	Huge personnel costs	Process oriented	Technocratic

Implications for American Schools

It is perhaps simplistic to characterize the inspectorate as a practitioner-based system of assessment focused on results, accreditation as an assessment system focused on process, and standards-based reform as an accountability system that relies solely on tests, but just to maintain clarity, those descriptions may do, for the moment. Each of these approaches brings with it some benefits and some drawbacks (table 9-2).

Accreditation is a relic of the time when the best and brightest could decide, behind closed doors, what was best for the masses. Perhaps the College of Cardinals is as secretive in its deliberations in a papal election as each of the eight regional accrediting bodies in the United States. Suddenly, a puff of white smoke signifies that a school has been accredited. But in the days of open government, closed deliberations are distasteful, serving adults' needs better than the students' needs. Standards-based reform is only marginally better. It appeals to a compulsion for precision and certitude felt by many policymakers but does little to respect the complex business of teaching and learning in real classrooms.

Under an inspectorate system, by contrast, the focus is on how well the schools *provide* for the needs of their students. Is the curriculum adequate? Is the school well managed? Do parents and students have a place to insist that their concerns be met? What is the ethos of the classroom? Is the local board encouraging real learning? Or has it operated under the assumption that these children cannot learn because they are immigrants or members of a minority group? These are very real questions that practically every school inspector raises sooner or later at most schools.

There can be little doubt, based on table 9-2, that of the three systems of evaluation, the inspectorate offers by far the most comprehensive benefits. Accreditation and standards-based reform, at least as implemented in the United States, come off at best as poor seconds. Equally clearly, the inspectorate as practiced in Britain is accompanied by huge personnel costs. It is highly unlikely that the United States as a whole, or any individual state, would want to run the political risks of advocating the development of a major new bureaucracy to oversee school improvement. (There are no political risks in criticizing American schools and plenty of political benefits in doing so. But promising to put real resources, human or financial, into the effort to fix schools is accompanied by nothing but risk in an antitax environment. In many ways, successive generations of politicians have been better served by the continuing existence of low-performing schools than they would be if they had been serious about fixing them.)

Experience in the United States

Of course, some states might be willing to develop an inspectorate of sorts, at least on an experimental basis. Indeed, several modest steps along these lines have been developed by school systems and states, and they might well serve as the foundation for a more formal effort to provide technical assistance under the No Child Left Behind legislation enacted in 2002.

As part of the renewal process of Massachusetts's first fourteen charter schools, for example, the state hired SchoolWorks, an independent consulting firm, to send teams of inspectors into each of the fourteen schools.[21] In many ways, the inspections that were developed tracked some of the best practices in Britain, as each team of inspectors was asked to assess progress toward important objectives, including improving student achievement and organizational and fiscal stability. Each team developed a renewal report on each school. According to the state, the renewal reports sound very similar to the expectations of the British inspectors: They should be "neither statistical nor empirical, but. . .a close, clear look at a school and its uniqueness by a team of seasoned practitioners."[22] The value of these reports, according to Kathryn Ciffolillo and Rebecca Wolf, is that they provide a "degree of objectivity that cannot be gained from within the school community."

Virginia is in the process of adopting a different approach, according to recent reports. Borrowing the corporate strategy of "turnaround specialists," the state plans to create an elite cadre of experienced principals with the skills to jump-start improvement in schools with poor performance records.[23] According to news accounts, the first ten principals will be chosen in the summer of 2004 to attend workshops jointly sponsored by the University of Virginia's education and business schools. They will then fan out, either as principals at individual schools or as advisers supporting the principals at these schools. The aim is to have the new specialists remain at a school for a three-year period.

Kentucky has the lengthiest experience with these efforts. Although not described as "inspectors," the *distinguished educator* program adopted as part of Kentucky's comprehensive Education Reform Act in 1990 (KERA) in many ways functioned as an inspectorate system. The program offered technical assistance to struggling schools from a cadre of outstanding educators. Schools designated as STAR schools (School Transformation Assistance and Renewal) were required to develop a school improvement plan, and they were eligible to receive funds for school improvement. They were also eligible to receive assistance from a "distinguished educator" (selected and trained by the Kentucky Department of Education). In the first two years of the program, particularly troubled schools were known as "crisis schools," and these schools were assigned two full-time distinguished educators with authority to evaluate all personnel and recommend removal of staff. After six months, the distinguished educators determined which of the certified staff should be retained, dismissed, or transferred.

Between 1994 and 1998, distinguished educators worked in some 230 schools in crisis.[24] An initial evaluation of the program found that teachers' embarrassment at being subjected to appraisal by a distinguished educator diminished quickly when the benefits of the relationship became apparent. Among other things, the technical assistance helped improve needs analysis and improvement planning, and professional development for teachers improved.[25] Perhaps most significantly, the intervention of the distinguished educator increased test scores and set schools on an improvement path that survived the exit of the distinguished educator: all fifty-three schools assisted in the first two-year cycle made significant gains on state assessments, with forty-three of the fifty-three continuing to show improvement two years later.[26] Of the 188 schools involved in the second cycle, 167 improved, with 85 exceeding their improvement targets. Distinguished educators did not use their authority to dismiss personnel in any of the nine crisis schools.

Starting in 1999, assistance was provided not by distinguished educators but by "highly skilled educators." This shift involved more than nomenclature. The new program embodied three major shifts in emphasis: the educators providing technical assistance no longer had authority to remove faculty; assistance was voluntary, not mandatory; and the assistance focused on the lowest performing schools (previously the STAR program had also included high-performing schools that declined).

Despite these changes, state technical assistance to struggling schools continues to be effective. A major ongoing evaluation indicated that after ten years, the technical assistance program continued to attract well-qualified candidates, whose work with schools helped improve academic audits, school leadership, planning, professional development, curriculum alignment, instructional practice, and test preparation.[27]

Experience in Massachusetts, Kentucky, and elsewhere bears directly on the school improvement provisions of the federal No Child Left Behind statute. Under No Child Left Behind, states must provide schools designated as "in need of improvement" with technical assistance to help them develop a two-year turn-around plan. Every student in such a school has the option of transferring out of the school. The statute seems to recognize that schools need assistance in developing this turn-around plan. If they knew what to do, presumably, they would already be doing it.

Whether known as inspectors, distinguished educators, or highly skilled educators, persons from outside the school providing high-quality technical assistance seem to be a new arrow in the standards-based accountability quiver.

Toward an American Inspectorate

Desirable though it might be to have every school in the United States receive such assistance, it is unlikely that any state will any time soon provide it. It is one thing for a state such as Massachusetts to provide for inspections for less than 1 percent of its schools (there were 1,868 public elementary and secondary schools in Massachusetts in 1999, according to the U.S. Department of Education).[28] But to increase that level of effort by a factor of 20 or 25, so that over five years every school in the state could be inspected, might be too much to expect.

Yet the potential benefits of such technical assistance are so attractive, based on Kentucky's experience, that something might be developed. This is even more true if the results from the forced march of standards-based accountability continue to be as disappointing as they have been. The need to find a way to obtain the strengths of an inspectorate without the deficiencies of a large bureaucracy is compelling. The reality is that although every school in the United States could probably benefit from the kind of rigorous assessment of school quality conducted in Britain, some schools require such an assessment more than others. If coverage of 100 percent of American schools is not possible, certainly the wit and the will could be found to provide for inspections of perhaps the 20 percent in greatest need.

If this 20 percent figure were selected, many of these schools, probably those with the greatest enrollment, will undoubtedly be found in large cities; but many of them are also going to be located in isolated, low-income, rural areas. Both kinds of schools are likely to be resource poor, if not in dollar terms, certainly in human resources.

Political and business leaders might find themselves well served if instead of cursing the darkness of poor school performance in the United States, they lit the candle of professional school inspections as a key element of the response. As Wilson points out, the purpose of knowing and judging the practice of schools is to improve the practice. The focus must be squarely on teaching and learning. Somehow American reformers, and the policymakers who have listened to their prescriptions, have convinced themselves that an easy route to school reform can be found through tests, assessment, and punitive ideas about what to do with recalcitrant teachers and administrators.

Learning takes place when talented teachers have a meeting of the minds with students on something substantive. Everything else is secondary. Teaching and learning are the important elements for reform. Intervening from the outside to improve teaching and learning by relying on performance measures is an attractive but in the end technocratic vision. What happens in real classrooms between adults and children is the key to reform. In the end, reformers and policymakers cannot continue their studious avoidance of what goes on inside individual schools and classrooms. Assessing whether a school is good or not in the United States will require, sooner or later, what Wilson says is required in England: we must send someone to visit it.

Notes

1. *School Inspections Act 1996* (London: Stationery Office, 1996).
2. "Introduction to OFSTED: HM Inspectors" (www.ofsted.gov.uk/about/inspinfo/hminspecthtm [May 2003]).
3. *Charter: HM Inspectorate of Education in Scotland* (London: Stationery Office, June 2001).
4. Starting with Victoria's nearly six-decade reign and ending with Elizabeth II, a queen has sat on the English throne for two-thirds of the time the system of inspectors has existed. Although a string of undistinguished kings filled in between these two women, the title adopted in Victoria's reign, "Her Majesty's inspectors," has held up well.
5. Kathryn Ciffolillo and Rebecca Wolf, *Renewal Findings: A Review of the First Fourteen Massachusetts Charter School Renewal Inspection Reports* (Boston: Pioneer Institute, n.d.).
6. Jan Battles, "Teachers Defy Union over Ban on School Inspectors," *Sunday Times* (London), August 19, 2001, p. 7.
7. The structure described is relatively new, adopted in 1992. Before 1992, HMIs were civil servants reporting to the secretary of education. They were an elite group within the Department of Education, encouraged to be part of the organization and to advise it, but to maintain their independence at the same time. About five times as many local inspectors were hired by local education agencies. These local inspectors were the seedbed for many of today's contract inspectors. See Thomas A. Wilson, *Reaching for a Better Standard: English School Inspection and the Dilemma of Accountability for American Public Schools* (Teachers College Press, 1996).
8. "Introduction to OFSTED" (www.ofsted.gov.uk/about/intro.htm [May 2000]).
9. "Her Majesty's Inspectorate of Education: About Inspections" (www.scotland.gov.uk.hmie/aboutinsp.htm [May 2000]).
10. "OFSTED Inspection Programme" (www.ofsted.gov.uk/about/inspecpr.htm [May 2000]).
11. "Mixed Report Card for Schools," *BBC News*, January 14, 2002.
12. *Officer for Standards in Education (OFSTED), Corporate Plan for Financial Year 2001–02* (London: Crown Copyright, 2001).
13. "Introduction to OFSTED, Regulatory Functions" (www.ofsted.gov.uk/about/reg.htm [May 2000]).
14. "Her Majesty's Inspectorate of Education: About Inspections" (www.scotland.gov.uk.hmie/aboutinsp.htm).
15. Wilson, *Reaching for a Better Standard*, p. 27.
16. Ibid., pp. 118–38.
17. Ibid., pp. 14–15.
18. "Commentary," *The Annual Report of Her Majesty's Chief Inspector of Schools*.
19. Wilson, *Reaching for a Better Standard*, p. 127.

20. *Independence, Accreditation, and the National Interest*, A Special Report on Accreditation from the National Policy Board on Higher Education Accreditation (Washington, 1994).

21. Ciffolillo and Wolf, *Renewal Findings*.

22. Ibid.

23. Jeff Archer, "Va. Principal Cadre Aims to Fix Schools," *Education Week*, April 28, 2004, p. 3.

24. Jane L. David, Patricia J. Kannapel, and G. Williamson McDiarmid, *The Influence of Distinguished Educators on School Improvement: A Study of Kentucky's School Intervention Program* (Lexington: Partnership for Kentucky Schools, 2000).

25. Ibid.

26. Ibid.

27. Jane L. David, Pamela Coe, and Patricia J. Kannapel, *Improving Low-Performing Schools: A Study of Kentucky's Highly Skilled Educator Program* (Lexington: Partnership for Kentucky Schools, 2003).

28. National Center for Education Statistics, *Digest of Education Statistics, 2000* (Government Printing Office, 2001), p. 118, table 97.

TEN   *Toward a*
       "Third Way"

PAUL T. HILL

JAMES HARVEY

SCHOOL DISTRICTS INEVITABLY focus on the here
and now. Constant demands for services from parents and pressures for
pay, benefits, and reduced workload from teachers almost always dominate the concerns of school boards and central offices.

In practical terms, this means that, despite lip service to the contrary,
most districts ignore reform. Deep and long-lasting reform strategies require forms of investment, monitoring, and adjustment that school districts have no history of providing. Commitment to change includes
monitoring leading indicators of whether reforms are happening as intended; reporting on real-dollar flow of funds; tracking the effectiveness
of individual schools, especially those educating low-income and minority pupils; incubating new schools and instructional programs; continu-
ously reviewing the quality of the human resource pool from which schools
draw; and investing in new recruitment and training mechanisms to attract the best possible people to lead and teach in the schools.

Few school districts take these functions seriously. Most discourage
close monitoring of reform implementation, publish summary budgets that
hide as much as they reveal about intradistrict flows of funds and differences in real-dollar spending from one school to another; avoid sharp judgments on the performance of individual schools; prefer continual tinkering
with troubled schools over their closure and reopening under new management; and leave the supply of teachers to the exigencies of the labor
market—and the supply of principals to self-starters who enter training

programs. The new institutions described in this book can help address these deficiencies.

Yet these institutions cannot create themselves. Local districts are unlikely to launch them. If they are to come into being, they will need to be financed by a combination of philanthropic and statewide or national initiatives. The vision of independent institutions to support school reform described in this volume is an expansive one. Few localities have any such institutions, and starting them in particular cities will demand organization and outlays. Although some school districts might put funds into some of these ideas, significant funding from district sources is unlikely. State governments might be able to invest more funds in starting and maintaining such institutions, but in the long run funding is more likely to come from local businesses and foundations.

Costs and Financing

The total cost of these institutions will be significant, but probably not more than the combined amount now spent for these functions by district central offices and local philanthropies. In Seattle, for example, one analysis of philanthropic giving estimated donations of nearly $150 per student.[1] Even if school systems received only one-third of that rate, a system the size of Chicago, Houston, or Los Angeles would receive private grants in excess of $20 million annually. These grants now support less productive initiatives than those suggested here, but, if thoughtfully reallocated and coordinated, the same amounts of money could easily pay to build vital new local capacities to sustain school reform.

Table 10-1 outlines the approximate costs of building and sustaining these institutions in a major metropolitan area. It shows the start-up costs of such institutions and the annual costs of supporting them. The start-up costs are predictable and have little to do with the size of the metropolitan area. Some of the annual operating costs, however, depend on district size and the ability of the new institutions to charge districts for the services they provide. Table 10-1 estimates continuing contributions needed from businesses and philanthropies in addition to fees.

The only item in table 10-1 whose costs exceed the normal philanthropic support for public education is the real estate trust. Much depends on how this is established and properties are transferred to its management. Skillful trust managers may be able to finance start-up by borrowing against the value of buildings or by capturing rental payments

Table 10-1. *The Cost of New Institutions*
Millions of dollars

What is needed to sustain reform	Start-up costs	Annual grant support
Civic oversight capacity	1.0	0.5
School incubator	1.0	10.0
Human resource development		
Teachers	1.0	0.5
Principals	1.0	0.5
Benefit providers	1.0	...
Real estate trust	5.0	...
Data analyst	1.0	10.0
School inspectorate	0.5	0.3

Source: Authors' calculations.

for buildings used by charter and private schools and businesses. However, the legal expenses of start-up, and the costs of creating building inventories and rehabilitating structures too dilapidated to be rented out, will impose significant front-end costs. In some communities these might all be borne by philanthropy.

Philanthropic Role

Such investments will require careful planning and collaboration among funders. Individual foundations or business philanthropies will have their own abilities and constraints. But philanthropies should encourage their grant officers to enter agreements with other funders in order to contribute to pooled funds for initiatives that no single funder can afford, financially or politically, on its own. Local philanthropies expecting public education to change should do no less themselves. They must open themselves to new and more challenging roles and to collaboration on initiatives that might discomfit traditionalists (in and out of the schools) and cause criticism.

National foundations and corporate philanthropies that wish to support school reforms in cities that are not their corporate headquarters, can help create these institutions in two ways. First, they can fund development of national prototype institutions that can develop materials and methods that can be used in all cities. The Annie Casey Foundation and the Atlantic Philanthropies have sponsored development of a national prototype school incubator at the University of Washington, and Casey is also supporting incubators in several cities. The Wallace Foundation has supported development of human resource monitoring institutions in this way, through a grant to the University of Washington's Center on Re-Inventing Public Education. National business groups sponsored development of New American Schools designs and related assistance organizations, which can help transform schools everywhere.[2] Second, national businesses and foundations can also join local coalitions and fund creation of local institutions, as the Chicago-based Joyce Foundation is starting to do in Cleveland and Milwaukee.

A "Third Way"

It is clearer today than ever before that philanthropy cannot ultimately be neutral toward policy. Philanthropic investments either buttress the existing system or put it under pressure to change. Efforts to help children and teachers directly—for example, by funding teachers' projects or supplementing children's learning outside school hours—often buttress the existing system by deflecting attention from its performance and compensating in various ways for the system's failures. Some philanthropists who have invested millions to transform individual schools are shocked to find that the system uses these schools not as models for the transformation of all schools but as Potemkin villages that are said to demonstrate the system's commitment to quality and reform while actually helping it fend off large-scale change. Such conclusions have led philanthropists like Reid Hastings, founder of Netscape, to invest in organizations to create charter schools rather than to work within school districts.

Serious efforts to improve existing public schools—for example, by creating new whole-school designs or promoting smaller schools—inevitably run afoul of district and union policies. Philanthropists such as the Annenberg or Gates foundations start out by professing a deep commitment to the cause—and the improvement—of public education. Still, they often find themselves at odds with the school board members, central office bureaucrats, and teachers union leaders who are the most prominent symbols—and power centers—of public education. Even philanthropies that try to help school districts and teachers unions transform themselves from within are often frustrated by the results. The Teachers Union Reform Network sponsored by the Pew Trusts and the Broad Foundation has been crippled by local union elections that rejected reform-minded leaders in three flagship cities: Seattle, Cincinnati, and Chicago. Business-funded New American Schools teams were abruptly kicked out of San Antonio when a new school board sponsored by dissident teachers fired the superintendent. Teachers' complaints led to the abandonment of Memphis's widely touted effort to use New American Schools designs to transform its public schools.

In this environment, what can philanthropies do? Should they continue to prop up a system that is not improving, either on its own or with the private funds invested in it? Or should they stop working with it altogether—as three local foundations in Pittsburgh did in 2003? Neither of these polar choices is necessary.

This chapter suggests a pair of approaches to philanthropy that can resolve this dilemma. The first approach emphasizes engagement with community leaders that goes well beyond the existing public school system. In pursuing this strategy, philanthropies must provide the initiative and leadership because the entities that make up what is usually considered the local school district—the school board, superintendent, and teachers union—are inherently unable to agree on a powerful reform strategy or to pursue any strategy rigorously or for a long time.

The second approach is to fund institutions and activities that are needed for fundamental school reform but that school districts and state agencies are not likely to support. School districts are so driven to meet demands for current services and salaries that they cannot invest in such important functions as tracking school performance, analyzing real-dollar flows of funds, starting new schools to replace failed ones, and providing facilities for alternative or innovative instructional programs.

These two approaches complement each other. Engagement with broader leadership groups means that philanthropists contribute to the development of powerful strategies to change the educational opportunities of tens of thousands of children. Funding activities that school districts will not or cannot support means that philanthropists can create options for students, including new schools, new forms of instructional support, and choices for families that the government system typically resists or marginalizes.

Taken together, these two strategies constitute a "third way" that allows philanthropists to help expand educational opportunities for children without depending on existing systems to do the right thing or turning their backs on existing institutions and structures of public education. The third way uses private funds to create environments in which all schools gain access to quality teachers and instructional programs. Educators and community leaders know how individual schools are performing, and parents have many options from which to choose. The third way uses private funds to help parents and community leaders judge school performance and take initiative on behalf of children in schools that are not teaching them what they need to succeed in American life.

In some respects, this "third way" for philanthropy benefiting education parallels the approach taken by third way politicians in the West, including "new Democrats" in the United States and "new Labour" in England. These political leaders have sought to advance public goals such as equal opportunity and full employment through new means that rely less heavily on government programs and more critically on private institutions, market forces, and choices for families and professionals. They see government as a promoter of options, a guarantor of baseline quality, and a source of information as much as finance, rather than simply as a monopoly provider. They have not given up on government. But neither are they satisfied with its traditional mechanisms.

Serious, lasting changes in the performance of big-city schools are unlikely if the supporters of public education limit themselves to whatever reform initiatives superintendents can muster. With history as our guide, we see that this strategy fails, often sooner rather than later. The third way seeks the goal of quality education for all children but seeks it by trying to move the existing system in desirable directions and by helping to create alternatives to it. Third way philanthropy does not confuse ends with means. It affirms the goals of public education—to ensure that all children learn what they need in order to become fully functioning citizens of our democracy and successful participants in a modern economy—and measures institutions against those goals. Institutions like school districts are valuable to the degree they attain those goals. Insofar as they fail to attain those goals, however, they must change.

The third way in a political sense is described by its advocates as a new sort of social compact, one that balances rights and responsibilities and helps citizens and communities solve their own problems. The third way recognizes that an entitlement mentality characterizes both the political right and left. On the right, reactionaries do not hesitate to demand such benefits as high-quality transportation systems, rising standards of living, and subsidized university education, while demonizing government and opposing the taxes that might pay for these benefits. On the left, zealots demand income security, protection from foreign competition, and high-wage jobs, while heaping contempt on the market-based economy that provides these benefits and ignoring the dynamics of how individual skills interact with effort and capital amid global pressures to produce economic growth. This new third way sets out to balance relationships among individuals, markets, and the government. Its ambitious goals include promoting equal opportunity for all while providing special privilege for none, encouraging an ethic of individual responsibility across the board, and designing new approaches to government that encourage public-private partnerships to help citizens help themselves.

Since the United States was created, an enduring issue has been the effort to resolve the question of the respective spheres of individuals, markets, and communities (and the state) in advancing the public good. In recent decades, the American educational answer has been that the state, in the form of local schools and public employees, was best equipped to provide educational services to American children—and everything ancillary to learning in the schools. There is a certain logic to that position, given that states compel students to attend school and are, hence, obligated to pay for schools.

But if there is a logic in favor of the state paying for educational services, there is no inherent logic to support the idea of public entities paying for ancillary services. The new institutions proposed in this book suggest that individuals, markets, and the larger community outside the schools have an equal stake in the success of schooling and can provide support for ancillary services outside the classroom. These services range from human resource development, leadership identification, and accountability systems to real estate management, civic and professional oversight, and data development. Just as it became self-evident during the 1930s that private markets could not begin to address every social need, so, too, did it become apparent in the 1990s that public solutions to every problem were neither efficient nor deft enough to respond to every public demand.

This third way philosophy, therefore, is a good fit with the needs of K–12 education in our big cities, where more than half the low-income and minority students now reach their eighteenth birthdays unable to read newspapers or function in jobs that require complex use of numbers. These outcomes have many causes, to be sure. But the fact relevant to philanthropy is this: in many urban neighborhoods, the existing public schools are failing to educate the children they are supposed to serve. In this situation, the goal of third way philanthropy is to help create settings in which children can learn. Whether to help existing schools or to support alternatives is a practical question, not an issue of principle. The schools that now exist (and the districts that provide them) warrant philanthropic support only insofar as they adapt to the needs of their students. Alternative arrangements must be measured against the same standard.

Individual analysts, policymakers, and philanthropists will no doubt find some of the ideas outlined in this volume more attractive than others. However, this book will have failed if they mistake the trees they do not like for the forest that needs to be developed. Public education in America's cities needs new community-based leadership, new strategies, and new investment. We have already tried leadership without strategy, strategy without investment, and investment with neither leadership nor strategy.

Today, forty years after the federal enactment of the Elementary and Secondary Education Act approaches, a third way beckons—an effort to harness leadership, strategies, and investment in the cause of improving learning for all.

Notes

1. Mary Beth Celio, *Random Acts of Kindness, External Resources Available to the Seattle Public Schools* (Seattle: Center on Reinventing Public Education, 1996).

2. See, for example, www.crpe.org; and www. naschools.org (June 2004).

Contributors

Sarah R. Brooks is an admissions officer at Carleton College.

Michael DeArmond is a research staff member at the Center on Reinventing Public Education, Daniel J. Evans School of Public Affairs, University of Washington.

James Harvey is a senior fellow at the Center on Reinventing Public Education, Daniel J. Evans School of Public Affairs, University of Washington.

Paul T. Hill is a nonresident senior fellow at the Brookings Institution and research professor at the University of Washington's Daniel J. Evans School of Public Affairs.

Marguerite Roza is research assistant professor at the University of Washington's Daniel J. Evans School of Public Affairs.

Abigail Winger is a freelance consultant from Milwaukee, Wisconsin.

Index

Outflows of teachers, 60
Outsider roles of principals, 69–70
Oversight. *See* Civic oversight

Parents, informing about reform
strategies, 23–24
Parochial schools, and headship role,
67–68
Peer support, 74–75, 80
Performance data analysis, 84–86,
87–88
Philanthropies, 42, 117–22
Planning, in start-up schools and
incubators, 45, 49
Policy, and philanthropy, 118
Politics, internal and external, 17–18
Portland Schools Real Estate Trust
(Oregon), 31–36
Principals: certification rules, 70; and
leadership development, 75–80;
role definition, 67–70; shortages,
65–66, 71–72; tracking supply of,
88; training, 77–78; unqualified,
71–72
Private schools, and headship role,
67–68
Profiles: districtwide, 92–94; school-
by-school, 90–92
Prototype institutions, national, 117–
18
Public Schools Real Estate Trusts,
31–38, 117
Purposes of schools, various, 4–5

Quality improvement movement, 3–4

Real estate management. *See* facilities
Real estate trusts, 31–38, 117
Recruiting: and flow management,
58–59; of principals, 74, 75–76,
79; and strategy monitoring, 94
Red Flag Schools, 91–92
Reform, strategic: changes required
for effectiveness in, 18; and civic
leadership groups, 20; and district
profiles, 93–94; and real estate

trusts, 37–38; terminating old
arrangements, 21–22; third way
philanthropy, 118–22. *See also*
Civic oversight
Reform initiatives, ephemeral, 12
Registered inspectors, 101
Regulatory relief, and civic oversight
groups, 22
Reinventing government initiatives,
3–4
Report cards, school, 84
Research departments, 95
Role definition for heads and
principals, 67–70, 75

Salaries, average vs. real, 88–89
School boards, 18, 20, 68–69
School districts: building management and ownership, 28–31;
control over principals, 68–69;
districtwide capacity profiles, 92–
94; human resource structures,
61; isolation of, 17–18; leadership
shortages caused by, 71–72;
philanthropic efforts vs. policy,
118–19; principal shortages, 65–
66; systemic resistance to focused
leadership, 66–67
School follow-up, in inspection
systems, 104
School-model development efforts, 6
School preferences, significance of,
91
Schools on the Rise, 91–92
Scott, Brian, 32
Seattle, 89–90, 91
Small schools, preference for, 43
Smith, Franklin, 26
Standards, in inspection systems, 104
Standards-based reform, and
inspectorates, 105–09, 112
STAR schools (School Transforma-
tion Assistance and Renewal),
110, 111
Start-up challenges for schools,
43–45

Start-up costs, 116–17
State support, and civic oversight
 groups, 22
Strategic performance data, 84–86
Strategic reform. *See* Reform,
 strategic
Student outcomes, 84–86, 87–88,
 102–03
Superintendents: early warning on
 schools, 90–91; facilities challenge, 26; human resource units
 reporting to, 61; turnover, and
 reform strategies, 18, 20–21. *See
 also* Leadership development
Systems of governance. *See* Governance systems

Teachers: career and shorter-term
 teachers, 53–54, 56–57; counseling out ineffective teachers, 60,
 88; induction and collaboration,
 59–60, 68, 69; labor market for,
 55–56; quantity vs. quality, 11–
 12; tracking supply and
 distribution of, 88
Teachers Union Reform Network,
 118
Teacher turnover and flow management: benefits, 56–57; costs, 117;
 induction and collaboration, 59–
 60; institutionalization of, 57–60;
 job mobility, 55; knowledge of
 subjects, 56; labor market, 55–56;
 outflows, 60; traditional hiring
 processes, 52; two-pathways

strategy, 53–54;
 uncompetitiveness of urban
 schools, 52–53
Teaching, collaborative, 59–60, 68,
 69
Technical capacities, 6, 44, 96
Third way philanthropy, 118–22
Training: developmental placements,
 74, 75–76, 79–80; just-in-time,
 74–75; in new leadership institutions, 77–79; principal's roles
 mismatched with, 69–70; university education departments, 76
Transitions between schools, 86
Trusts, real estate, 31–38, 117
Turnaround specialists, 110
Two-pathways strategy, 53–54

Union policies, 118–19
University education departments, 76
Urban schools, uncompetitiveness of,
 52–53

Vining, Aiden, 30
Virginia, 110
Visitation, in inspection systems, 103

Wallace Foundation, 118
Washington State Processing
 Cooperative (WSIPC), 96
Weimer, David, 30
Wilson, Thomas A., 103–04, 105,
 112
Wise, Arthur, 53
Wolf, Rebecca, 109–10